Wish List

Heather Hair

Psalm 40:1-3

Interior Design: Jordan Jamison

Cover Design: H Publishing

Edited by: Gabe Smith, ThM

ISBN-13: 978-1-949627-02-2
ISBN-10: 1-949627-02-0

CONTENTS

CHAPTER 1: THE UNICORN IN THE ROOM

It all started with a unicorn and a rainbow.

A simple idea. I had learned over time that when we pray, we should be mindful of the attitude and spirit in which we pray. Always pray from a position of gratitude and joy rather than desperation and lack. Gratitude and joy demonstrate faith. And God adores faith.

Faith is God's love language.

The idea in prayer is to get creative—have fun with it. Prayer doesn't have to be ritualistic, boring or even all that religious. God is real. Talk to Him like He is real. Talk to Him like you know Him, and you'll be surprised how much He then makes Himself known. Do whatever you need to do to give yourself a mindset of happiness and hope when you pray. Then sit back and watch Him move mountains on your behalf.

Knowing this and having experienced it for some time, I decided to apply it to a situation at work a few years ago. It was a situation bigger than me. Bigger than any of us. But it was something I wanted for us as an organization. So I asked myself before creating my prayer strategy, "What makes me happy? What will immediately put me in that mindset?"

It didn't take long for me to come up with a lot of things, actually. My kids, friends, traveling, watching football, pizza, being in nature—to name a few. Yet these things also often come with the realities of living life in an imperfect world. Despite their greatness, they just do. These negative realities can attach mental or emotional undercurrents of bad things to the good. So while there is joy, there is also loss. While there is happiness, there is also hurt.

Knowing this, I sat before my empty prayer strategy page—stumped.

My happy list had come with mixed emotions. I'm sure all of ours do. This is because with good comes struggle. It's in the DNA of being human. That's why I decided in order for me to get the right mindset for this all-too-larger-than-life prayer request, I would have to go outside of what is merely human.

Thus—the unicorn.

And the rainbow, of course.

Unicorns and rainbows typically go hand in hand. And unicorns and rainbows typically produce immediate thoughts of happiness, gratitude and beauty in me. For whatever reason, I see no way that either of those two things can ever go wrong. At least not in my, quite youthful, imagination. So that's what I decided to use in my prayer strategy at work—a unicorn and a rainbow.

Why did I need this strategy?

Because I had opened my big mouth a few years earlier in even bigger faith.

Faith is God's love language.

Nearly a decade ago, I found myself in my first year at this job for a prominent pastor—a job I enjoyed and one that definitely stretched me. Upon his recruiting of me to create both a marketing and development department for his national organization, he asked me where we would be in five years. What was my projection for our growth?

At the time I confidently, albeit naively, told him we would grow 150% by year five. Yes, I made that claim with no plan and no experience in non-profit management. I boldly proclaimed we would more than double our annual income in those five years to an amount this three-decade-old organization had never even come close to. I said it to him as if it were so. No hesitation. No doubt.

To make matters worse, I made this claim during the heart of the national economic downturn. This is when in business and non-profit worlds a flat annual income was considered the new "up" in growth. Simply *not* losing money each year was thought to be a positive thing. Most non-profits were laying off staff, cutting ministry initiatives, and slashing budgets. But that didn't daunt me. We were not only going to grow, I told him confidently— but we were going to grow immensely.

Did I have any idea how?

Not a clue.

Did I have any staff given to work with?

Not a one.

A budget?

Not much.

But none of that mattered. I could feel this goal in my spirit. I believed this wasn't my goal, but, rather, it was God's goal for where He wanted to take this impactful ministry. God wanted it to grow because in its growth, God could use it to bless more people. It just made sense to me. So I said it out loud.

Plus I had seen God move enough times in miraculous ways throughout my life that I recognized His heart when it beat in cadence with my own.

This wasn't *my* lofty idea. I truly believed it was His.

A Rainbow on the Wall

Three years into my five-year projection, and despite learning all I could about non-profit management and new marketing approaches, we were not even close to the pace to reach my goal. We had grown, yes. I had been given a few staff by then, which proved helpful. But my goal had been set too high for humanity's hand anyhow. My goal didn't even register on the trajectory of healthy growth levels for non-profits. A healthy non-profit is supposed to grow 10% a year. I had projected 150% in five. Sure, we had reached around 40% after two years, but my really high goal taunted me as, "Insane. Crazy. Impossible. Are you serious, Heather?"

So, needless to say, things didn't look all that good entering my third year.

But my spirit still said yes. My goal would come about.

I just didn't know how.

That's when I decided to increase my prayer strategy for this goal. Life *is* spiritual, but it's easy to forget that truth in our man-made surroundings. Yes, in Africa, where I had lived for nearly the entire decade before— taken away from our human safety nets, I knew life was spiritual on a daily basis. But here in America, it's easy to think that what we achieve or become is largely dependent on our own efforts. We forget how important prayer really is.

I admit I had forgotten it in those first two years at this non-profit while I spent most of my time working my fingers to the bone. I had let faith slide and replaced it with effort. I thought it was all up to me to produce this growth. But I wasn't going to let that mindset continue. So I emailed my graphic designer and asked him to put a certain number I had chosen on a large page and print it for me.

"Make it look 'happy,'" I said.

He didn't. It came back incredibly boring and bland. Just a black number on a white background. Apparently my creative direction had been lost in communication. I couldn't blame my designer, though. How do you make a number look happy anyhow?

That's when I walked over to his desk and said, "Well, could you at least make the number bigger? And put a unicorn and a rainbow on it, too."

My designer looked at me with one of those blank stares I sometimes get from adults. His look didn't faze me, though, so I held my own and continued, "Well, can you?"

He nodded and mumbled something that resembled agreement. I walked away, not saying much of anything else either. A day or two later, I got my poster-sized number designed with the bright colors of a rainbow and a pink unicorn right smack in the middle of it. Perfect! Well... perfectly incredulous, that is. I felt a little childish holding it. Even more so when I considered what I was going to have to do with it now that I had it—which was to hang it smack dab in the middle of my wall in my office just facing my desk.

Would other adults see it when they came in? Yes.

Would they also have that blank stare adults sometimes give me? Yes.

Would they question whether or not to bring up the unicorn in the room? Again, yes.

My poster became a point of attention over the course of the next few months. I tried my best to explain that I had hung it there as a reminder to pray happily for the financial goal I had chosen for our growth that year. That was the number I had put on the poster. It was also a number we had never reached in the 30-year history of the organization. And it was a number we were not anywhere on pace to reach when I made my poster.

I couldn't quite tell which was more alarming to those who saw it—the number I had chosen or the pink unicorn displayed with it. It didn't matter. The responses were all the same.

"That's great, Heather, really great," my co-workers would say when eyeing my unicorn poster projection.

Then they would all somehow make their way quickly to my door to leave. After which I would hear laughter in the hall. No, I don't think I earned respect points for hanging up my unicorn and my rainbow. And I am absolutely certain Sheryl Sandburg would never endorse this idea for a woman in the workplace in *Lean In, Part 2*.

But I did bring some entertainment to the office and some variety to the water cooler talk. And at the end of the day, I reminded myself that my poster wasn't for them anyhow. Plus, the rest of my office looked as it ought. This poster was for me—and it was there to serve as a nudge to pray toward my financial goal for us as an organization in a spirit of happiness, expectation and gratitude.

See, it is the spirit in which we pray that embodies our faith. Yet we rarely pay attention to something as important as that. Think about it though. If your kid asked you to take him to a movie in a demanding, upset, entitled or even robotic manner, would that communicate much to you? Or what if he asked you to take him to a movie and then went out with some friends to get some dinner, or even went back to bed. You'd figure, like I would, that he had changed his mind and didn't want to go to the movie anymore.

> *It is the spirit in which we pray that embodies our faith.*

Or how about when your son runs up, gives you a big hug, and jumps up and down with excitement because he knows you're going to take him to a movie, and then asks. What then? You'd probably go.

I don't know why, but too often we make God into a machine.

God has a heart, like we do.

God has emotions. Lots of emotions.

God *is* love.

And He created us for relationships with Himself and each other. He wants to hear from us as we want to hear from those we love.

He is our Savior, yes, but He is also our friend.

This is why I reminded myself in this prayer strategy to pray from a place of delight.

And this is also why not long after I had hung up my prayer poster that I actually stopped praying about it altogether. Something inside of me had let me know that my prayer had been answered. And it was a "yes."

This moment of knowing was not an exceptional moment by any means. There were no angels singing to me. No real unicorn appeared in my office. God didn't show up visibly and hand me a special stick with super powers. I just... *knew*.

It's kind of like that feeling you get when you order bird food online, or whatever it is you order. You get the email receipt in your inbox. You read the delivery confirmation date. You know it will come. You give it no second thought. You're simply happy because what you have chosen will arrive.

So you rest.

This is exactly what I did regarding my financial projection. When I saw my poster from that point on, my spirit simply whispered... thanks.

Fast forward to the end of the year.

Did we hit my financial goal? You better believe we did! In fact, we surpassed it.

And while it was a surprise to everyone else on staff, it was no surprise to me. That year would end up being our highest annual percentage growth we had ever known.

And about those people who had been laughing outside my door when I first hung up my unicorn and rainbow—well, they weren't laughing anymore.

Let's just say no one has ever made fun of my rainbows or my unicorns since then. In fact, the following year I was asked by several co-workers, including my boss, what number I was going to put up this time. I saw the curiosity in their eyes, half wanting to joke but also half believing what had happened because they had experienced it themselves. They had witnessed it.

What was impossible to man was possible to God. So the next year I made another poster with a brand new number that would keep us on pace to hit my five-year projection. And the next year, we surpassed my number again.

But yes, you are right. This isn't a book about business—it's a book on prayer. However, I needed to set the stage with one of the more colorful illustrations in my life *on* prayer. This history is important before we get into the prayers that God does *not* answer and how that should impact your wish list. I've gotten a lot of prayer requests answered historically. But when it came down to it – they were usually not the ones I cared most deeply about. When I started to look at the prayers that I cared most deeply about and wonder why God didn't answer those the way I hoped, it began to inform those prayers more strategically. In fact, those *unanswered* prayers stood out so drastically to me begging me to ask, "What am I doing wrong, God?"

But before I get to the deeply-cared about unanswered prayers, let me share briefly about some answered ones first – for context.

Yahtzee, Diapers and Meat in the Mail

Faith and prayer have always come naturally to me in many ways. I'm that mom who says to her college-aged daughter while playing Yahtzee, "I'm asking God for five 3's and being grateful for them ahead of time," and then rolls five 3's in the very next toss. True story. My daughter then shrieks and screams, "Magic!" while yelling to her brother down the hall, "Mom's doing magic!" all the while with a look of horror and shock on her face.

And faith is like magic in many ways.

Faith evokes miracles. That's the whole point of faith. We sometimes forget that God wants to amaze us. He wants to show off. He wants to give us miracles in our everyday lives.

I'm also that uber-poor seminary-student wife with three kids under the age of six, who learned to pray with them for specific things like jelly and syrup. I had the flour. I had the oil. I could make the pancakes. But I had nothing to put on it for them. And no money to buy it. Not even a dollar. So we prayed. We asked God for jelly and syrup, only to have a neighbor less than a day later walk outside to get her mail at the same time I was getting mine and yell over, "Do you need some jelly and syrup?"

She had just finished up a weekend military expedition. She couldn't stand to see the leftovers go to waste so she had brought bags of the little packets of syrup and jelly home with her.

And no, I had never met this neighbor before.

And also no, she had no clue about our prayer.

But God did.

I'm also that mom who couldn't afford circus tickets for her kids but wanted so much to give them an experience so I told the family I would just ask God for them. Why not? God isn't opposed to circus tickets. He's not too busy to make our hearts laugh.

In the very week that I asked Him, another neighbor stopped by to see if we wanted circus tickets. They had seen our kids playing in the yard, and their employer handed out circus tickets every year to the employees for free. They didn't feel like going this year so they thought we might enjoy them.

They were right. We did.

You name it; I asked for it. As specific as I needed to

be—$35 for milk and diapers only to have exactly $35 show up the next day through a marketing survey request to taste pizza. (Food and money - bonus!)

I've asked for a computer more than once, and gotten it—both times within a week. I've asked for oranges and underwear. Gotten both. I've asked for meat. The meat, funny enough, came in the mail. Some friend three states away felt led to order a honey baked ham and send it to us the very week I prayed with the kids for meat.

Like I said, we didn't have much money when we started as a young family. My first child came when I was only 18. And we definitely didn't have much when we moved to Africa. The first decade of scarcity as a young wife and mom prepared me for the next decade of a much higher level of dependence in Africa. Facing tropical sickness after tropical sickness with the closest qualified doctor an eight-hour drive away—God became very personal.

He had to.

Those were my babies.

And when your babies get malaria, typhoid, amoebas and whatever else time after time after time, you must take God seriously—quickly. When you have witchcraft and curses put on you, your family, your car and your pets, you find out how to access God's greater powers. You have to. You are forced to talk to Him as you would your pastor, your best friend, your father, your spouse, your mother, your doctor and anyone else.

When God is all you have, you get to know Him really well.

Through those decades, I learned to pray as if it were a normal part of life. I learned to pray for big things and small. From cups of coffee, to a car (twice), to a brand new home. Each time, without fail, the coffee, the car and the house came about, even with the details I had asked for specifically like color or model or flavor or floors.

I've prayed to see a giraffe when we're driving in Kenya, or rainbows when we would be playing inside. Even though it looked sunny outside, I needed some encouragement for that day so I prayed for a rainbow with the kids. And, as always, when I've had the faith and courage to tell those I love about these prayers ahead of time, God brought them about. Without fail. He put the rainbows in the sky, the giraffes beside the road, the coffee in my hand. I learned over and over that prayer works because I saw it work.

And, yes, I also learned that sometimes prayer *is* work. And sacrifice.

In Kenya, I was taught by so many spiritual giants— my Kenyan friends—how to connect the art of fasting with prayer – real fasting, not from social media, a television show or one meal. My Kenyan friends would fast for me when a child of mine was sick or I was discouraged by the challenges of living in a developing country amidst so much pain. For days on end, they fasted.

And that's not just Kenya. I recently went through a tough decision I had to make while also being assigned a difficult writing job, with less than a week to complete it. Knowing I was low on emotional energy, a dear friend here in the States offered to fast for me the entire time from all food until I finished the project. And she did. That motivated me to get it done in four days so my poor friend could eat!

I have also fasted for days for friends myself. One in particular struggled with a health issue for over a year, and he only seemed to be getting worse. The doctors were at a loss for making any improvements in his condition. So I shared with him that I would fast and pray for an entire week, just for his condition. Within a day of fasting, the extremity of his problem went down by half, and then by the next day down to only a fourth of what it had been. Now years later, it has not come back at all.

Prayer is one of the kindest gifts we can give each other.

I believe in prayer, deeply. I use it. Regularly.

Prayer moves mountains and changes hearts. And prayer done in the right spirit of gratitude and expectation is all the more powerful.

But I am not successful at prayer in every area of life.

I am not.

And it bothers me, deeply.

I have not cornered the market on this skill. At all.

I have not proven myself a master at prayer in every situation.

Depending on the request, I still get no reply.

In particular, one area has proved to be the most defeating to me. What makes this all the worse is that this particular area—outside of my kids—is the most important and valued area in my life.

It has been difficult to experience ongoing defeat here coupled with a feeling of powerlessness to change. So in the face of yet another failure and disappointment in this area a few years back, I decided to try and figure out why on earth it was so easy for me to have my prayers answered—however enormous or small—in other areas, but in this particular one, I was always striking out.

No matter what I did, no matter how many days and weeks I fasted, no matter how many people I recruited to pray for me, no matter how many Bible verses I read, how many sins I confessed or how long I hung out in the war room on my knees, I could not get my prayers answered when it came to this one area of my life.

And by "answered," I mean resolved.

There are always three answers to every prayer: Yes, no or wait.

Prayer isn't casting a wish to a cosmic genie for everything we want. God is sovereign and has full control over what He chooses to do. But when we pray and the answer is "no" or "wait," then, based on His Word, that answer should also come with the ability to handle it well, especially if we've asked for that ability. He promises to supply all we need when we are in alignment with Him.

Yet in this one area of my life, I was getting an awful lot of "nos" and "waits" and yet my inner turmoil, angst and inability to handle those "nos" and "waits" remained. The desire for a "yes" was just as strong as ever. So I found myself in a constant state of want. Disappointment. Longing. Confusion about what to do.

What do you do when prayer gets no reply?

What do we do when prayer gets no internal emotional or spiritual resolution?

Well, we often excuse it, justify it—explain it away. Because to acknowledge it would be akin to acknowledging the proverbial elephant in the room (or unicorn, in my case). It's not something we like to do. The entirety of our relationship with God rests on our trust in Him.

To say that He is not trustworthy or His Word has not come through is to upset that delicate balance which we call belief. Many of us try to ignore this reality similar to ignoring the elephant in the room simply because it is not something we want to consider.

Yet because God is so clear on what He has said regarding prayer, and because I have seen Him move so quickly and so personally in my life in so many countless other ways, I couldn't ignore the fact that my prayers in this area kept going unresolved.

I had to get to the bottom of this.

I had to unearth why a unicorn would work so well for business but four weeks of fasting would not work at all for this other area in my life.

What was it about this unicorn that made it so magical? Why did rainbows produce results? How come something so simple as wishing for a Yahtzee met with no resistance at all? Yet something else so deeply-desired never seemed to get so much as a response.

The secret to the answer, I would soon discover, was not what I had expected at all.

The unicorn and the rainbow were nice, but, in the end, they were not the true catalyst. They were not the trick that got my prayers answered (and yes, I completed my fifth year with this non-profit, and we did surpass my goal of 150% growth, amazingly enough).

But tricks are not really what works when it comes to prayer.

Despite how adorable that unicorn truly is, the unicorn did nothing at all. What the unicorn represented, though, hovering beneath the layers of my hope—*that* was the true spark. That was what made the progression in my prayer from desire to result. And that was one (of several) thing(s) I did *not* have in this other area of my life, despite all of my best efforts to *will* myself to have it.

This "one thing" is the first reason why our prayers get no reply.

Sometimes we simply cannot *will* ourselves to believe. We just can't. Can you?

Are there things in your life that are easy to believe when you pray for them? Those are the things in which you see God come through for you over and over again.

And yet are there other things in your life that despite reading all the verses, saying all the affirmations, spending all the hours on your knees and speaking all the words of belief—deep down in your soul you really – just – don't - believe.

Tricks are not really what works
when it comes to prayer.

You doubt. Maybe because this desire—this wish—is too tender for you. Maybe this desire is *too* desired by you. Or this disappointment, were you to not get it, would be too painful for you.

So you pray a safe prayer, instead.

You, like so many of us, pray, "God—if it's your will... *blah, blah, blah and blah*, please." Fill in the blanks. You're afraid to believe and trust on this one.

I understand.

I'm also afraid to believe and trust on *this* one. We all have our own "this ones."

Maybe it's your health. It could be a financial struggle. It could be emotional wounds from a childhood pain. It could be your marriage. It could be romance. Even work. A wayward child. Or it could be a dream you've cradled for so long in the depths of your soul that it's covered only in cobwebs and dust. A dream you don't even dare speak of anymore.

Those are the prayers you and I wrestle with.

Those are the victories that don't come about so suddenly at all.

Those are the wars we wage often without so much as knowing how.

But those are also the wars we *must* learn to fight—and fight well—because our deepest desires are what will bring us our deepest delights. And Satan wants nothing more to keep us from just that. He wants to keep us from the abundance of God's provision and life.

So, my friend, I am with you in these longings we all share. Call them what you will. They are the things that make our hearts smile and our hopes fulfilled. But they are also the things that often elude us, just out of reach.

Just beyond our prayers.

CHAPTER 2: FAITH, TRUST & PIXIE DUST

My youngest daughter performed in a local production of Peter Pan a few years back. Peter Pan is a classic, and I enjoyed every minute of it. One of my favorite scenes has always been when Wendy and her brothers first learn how to fly. Peter tries to explain to them how easy it is to fly. They can do it simply by thinking happy thoughts.

"All you need is a little faith, trust and pixie dust," Peter says, with a grin on his face. Happy thought after happy thought enters the children's minds, and, within no time, they are flying high.

If only prayer were that simple.

But, actually, it is.

God has told us repeatedly in His Word that all we need is faith and trust. In fact, He's told us that we don't even need that much—a mustard seed will do. We bring the mustard seed; He adds pixie dust. Easy-peasy, according to God:

> Truly, I say to you, whoever says to this mountain, "Be taken up and thrown into the sea," and does not doubt in his heart, but believes that what he says will come to pass, it will be done for him. Therefore I tell you,

whatever you ask in prayer, believe that you have received it, and it will be yours. (Mark 11:23-24)

He said to them, "…For truly, I say to you, if you have faith like a grain of mustard seed, you will say to this mountain, 'Move from here to there,' and it will move, and nothing will be impossible for you." (Matthew 17:20)

And Jesus said to him, "'If you can'! All things are possible for one who believes." (Mark 9:23)

Ask, and it will be given to you; seek, and you will find; knock, and it will be opened to you. For everyone who asks receives, and the one who seeks finds, and to the one who knocks it will be opened. (Matthew 7:7-8)

Now to him who is able to do far more abundantly than all that we ask or think, according to the power at work within us. (Ephesians 3:20)

And this is the confidence that we have toward him, that if we ask anything according to his will he hears us. (1 John 5:14)

And Jesus answered them, "Truly, I say to you, if you have faith and do not doubt, you will not only do what has been done to the fig tree, but even if you say to this mountain, 'Be taken up and thrown into the sea,' it will happen. (Matthew 21:21)

And whatever you ask in prayer, you will receive, if you have faith. (Matthew 21:22)

For nothing will be impossible with God. (Luke 1:37)

Commit your way to the Lord; trust in him, and he will act. (Psalm 37:5)

Then Jesus answered her, "O woman, great is your faith! Be it done for you as you desire." (Mathew 15:28a)

And Jesus answered them, "Have faith in God." (Mark 11:22)

If you abide in me, and my words abide in you, ask whatever you wish, and it will be done for you. (John 15:7)[1]

Faith. Trust. That's all we need to not only move the mountains in our lives but to also apparently bring down any unwanted fig trees, raise the dead, walk on water and basically have everything we wish. He did say, "Ask whatever you wish," after all. And most of us do. But like the penny tossed into the shopping mall fountain, those wishes wind up silently drowning beneath ripples of doubt.

This is the same doubt that made it impossible for Wendy to fly once she became an adult. It's not an evil, sinister doubt by any means. It doesn't entail walking around entirely angry, bitter and jaded. Rather, it's an awareness of reality—what our five senses and experiences have taught us each and every day. It is doubt designed to protect us from potential disappointment. Doubt drafted by what we see, hear and expect.

---

[1] All verses in this section are taken from the ESV.

Peter has come back for Wendy. The pixie dust is still available for her to use. All Wendy has to do is think those same happy thoughts she had done once before and she could go on another grand adventure.

But Wendy knows better by now. She knows even happy thoughts would come with the stuff of life—realities of hurt, limitations and challenges. She knows by now that unicorns are not actually real, and neither are mermaids, and anything she tries to think about to bring pure joy has somehow been tainted by an internal awareness that things don't always turn out as we had hoped.

Maybe you've experienced something similar?

It's okay to admit it.

Faith. Trust. That's all we need to move the mountains in our lives.

Have you ever gotten that *off* feeling when things seem to be going really well, for far too long? It's just an uneasiness we do to ourselves to somehow brace our hearts and our minds in case things take a turn for the worse. It's the buffer we unknowingly erect around the things we desire most.

If you have ever felt this or done this, you're not alone. Most of us experience this, regularly. We may not recognize it because most of us don't walk around analyzing ourselves all the time. But we will catch it in moments, if we pay attention even slightly—especially those moments punctuated by delight, love and good things.

For example, have you ever caught yourself gazing at

your beautiful sleeping child as she dozes off to dream, feeling completely content and satisfied? And then all of a sudden a doubt creeps in. Will she be safe? Will I lose her one day? How would I handle that if I did? What does this world have in store for her, and how can I protect her from that pain? You walk out of the room no longer in the contentment you once held while standing there. You walk out with a mixture of what most would describe as an unsettledness, or even low-level fear.

Or have you ever found yourself sharing that loving look with your significant other and sensed a deep level of knowing—a warmth—only to have a very different feeling follow—almost immediately, almost instinctively? "Will this relationship last like this?" you wonder without really wondering at all. This thought is practically at the spirit level, deep in the sub-conscience of our soul. Our bodies recognize it and often respond physically and emotionally without our minds even being aware. Questions creep up such as: Does she really love me? What if he betrayed me? How would I handle that? Could I even handle that? A sea swirls in the abyss within you, muddling the initial feeling you first shared.

Or what about the project you completed at work that gained you so much admiration and attention and productivity for the business, or school or wherever you work? Have you ever caught yourself enjoying thoughts of achievement and satisfaction only to have hints of concern creep in about whether you can repeat it, or will things go backwards now? Or will what you just accomplished even last? Will your peers and boss hold you to too high of an expectation moving forward and you'll disappoint them after this? You smile when they praise you for the accomplishment, but your gut doesn't join you in that smile—not entirely.

Have you ever walked through your new home or new apartment with utter joy, thrilled with your decision and grateful for the new place you have—only to have a seed planted and wiggle around annoyingly in your soul? Will you be able to keep the house or apartment? What happens if you or your spouse has an accident or loses a job, or gets sick and can no longer work in order to pay the bills?

If you answered yes to any of those, which most, if not all, of us will have answered yes, you are not alone. We are not alone. We are all human. We do these things, think these thoughts, erect these walls because deep down inside something has taught us that good things cannot go on forever. Perhaps it's a carryover from Adam and Eve who lived a life of blissful peace and luxury only to be quickly uprooted and even more quickly booted out of the garden. Perhaps their intrinsic fears trickled down to us through our own inherited DNA. Who knows? However we got it or learned it, it exists. Within each of us exists an awareness that life is frail, love is fragile, health is never promised and ongoing peace is often a priceless carrot we seek but to little avail.

Life is our master teacher—and one of her most-taught lessons involves instructing us how not to trust. We learn like Wendy does, over time—gradually.

We learn to *grow up*.

God knows that. Jesus knows that. That's why He specifically told us to "become like little children" or we could not fully enter into the richness of His kingdom on earth (Matthew 18:3). Jesus made this analogy so clear because He knew that our doubts, suspicions and self-preservations would hold us back from belief.

He knew that a faith to move mountains had to be pure. Like a child's.

He also knew that very few of us, as adults, would have that kind of faith at all.

At least not in all areas of our lives.

Some of us have great faith in certain areas and no faith in others. I have no idea why I have childlike faith when it comes to certain things like business or tangible items. Perhaps ignorance is bliss, as they say, and when it comes to believing that God can do things for me on a lot of levels in those areas, I'm there. I believe. I'm ignorant to what could possibly stand in the way, go wrong or why I shouldn't get what I just asked for and worked toward.

Life is our master teacher—and one of her most-taught lessons involves instructing us not to trust.

But seeing this contrast between my answered prayers in those places and my unanswered prayers in certain relationships taught me something. It taught me a number of things, actually. One of the first things was that **the deeper my felt need is within my desire—in other words, the more dependent I feel upon the answer itself—the less faith I have for it.**

For example, had our business' bottom line not improved the 150% in five years, would I have been devastated? Probably not. I had no real emotional investment in our growth, just a wish. Or had I not gotten the exact color and model of the car that someone decided to give me a few years ago—had they chosen a different color and model since I hadn't even told them what I wanted anyhow—would this have challenged my faith and thrown me into the depths of depression? I doubt it. I wanted the car but the health of my heart wasn't dependent upon it.

Or how about that Yahtzee or cup of coffee? Or that meat in the mail? All of those things were nice, yes. But none of those things were truly needed. None of those things, if not answered, would have sent me into a tailspin of emotional vulnerability.

In fact, **the less I feel I need the answer to my prayer, the easier it is to believe I will receive it.**

Read that line again. Go ahead. It's important.

Now, ask yourself: Can you see a correlation of that truth in your own prayer life? The prayers you pray that you are less tied to their outcome—do they seem to get answers more quickly than the rest? How about the ones you toss up without much thought at all? Do they seem to "work better" than the ones you spend a good deal of time with on your knees? I can get excellent parking spaces all day long by thinking a quick little prayer simply because I'm just not highly invested in the outcome. So my faith is there.

Yet the more I feel I need whatever the answer to my prayer is, the harder it seems to have the faith to support that prayer.

Maybe it's the same for you. Maybe not. But I have a feeling it is. I have a feeling it's the same for all of us.

Yet, as with that elephant (or unicorn) in the room, we rarely want to admit it or talk about it. It doesn't sound very spiritual at all. We're told to pray. We sing songs about praying. We try to pump ourselves up by reminding ourselves that prayer will change everything. We watch movies on prayer. And prayer definitely has the potential and power to change everything.

But far too often, we've seen our own prayers go

unanswered or—worse yet—felt like they didn't get heard at all. The addiction remains. The depression lingers. The loneliness goes unresolved. The child stays distant. The marriage or dating relationship grows even more stagnant, empty or even controlling. The credit cards pile high. The health problems get worse. Or we keep clocking in at the same meaningless job.

The less I feel I need the answer to my prayer, the easier it is to believe I will receive it.

When this happens enough times in life, you and I begin to pray guarded prayers. We still pray, yes. I'm not saying we stop praying altogether. After all, we are Christians, and we go to church and post spiritual inspirations on our social media sites. Prayer is as Christian as apple pie is American.

The difference, though, is we now say prayers with parameters.

We erect conditions around what we truly want because if God doesn't provide—like He didn't the last time and even the time before that, we need a way to let Him off the hook. We need to keep our spiritual hope in tact. We need to set up that buffer between our trusting hearts and what might wind up being another deeply painful disillusioning disappointment.

But safe prayers don't work. Remember?

It's faith that moves mountains. Not precaution.

And even if safe prayers do appear to work at times, their outcome is usually temporary—leading to yet another reversal of hope.

As a reminder, I'm not talking about always getting your way in prayer, or always getting a "yes" answer. I'm talking about those times when you've prayed for something and the answer has been "no" or "wait," but you also did not receive the grace nor the peace to handle that "no" or "wait" well. Or you did not have the desire you were praying for removed *as* a desire, which sometimes also happens as an answer to prayer. That's what I mean by unresolved. I'm talking about those prayers that continue to leave us unsettled in their answer in many ways.

Twice Happens

I wouldn't have been forced to examine this myself, like I mentioned in the last chapter, except something happened in two back-to-back scenarios that, when compared together, just didn't add up. I've learned enough in reading the Bible to pick up on and pay attention to those times when something happens twice. God will often use "twice" to get our attention. Whenever Jesus would say, "Verily, verily," or "Mary, Mary," or anything twice—it meant, "Pay attention."

Gideon stuck his fleece out twice in order to receive a confirmation from God. Peter warmed his hands over a charcoal fire twice, once in betraying Christ and once in hearing his calling from Him. Joseph told Pharaoh that "twice" the matter was confirmed in his dream about the plenty and the famine.

When something happens once, it might be significant or it might not. But when something very similar happens twice, my friend, pay attention. That's God talking. That's God trying to confirm, guide, direct or answer you in a way He wants you to finally understand if you will just slow down and pay attention—to the *twice*.

Mine was a near empty nest by the time my *twice* happened. Three of my kids were college-aged and up, and the youngest split her time between me and her dad, along with his new wife. I had spent many years as a stay-at-home mom during my adulthood, homeschooling the kids for 11 of those years. As you can imagine, I was not used to being alone in a near-empty nest. I was not used to a quiet house or even making personal decisions based on what I wanted anymore (any mom can understand immediately what I mean by that.) Both my time and my choices had always been funneled through the framework and filter of others. Having had my first child at 18, my mindset had been shifted for as long as I could remember, and certainly as long as I had been an adult.

So becoming single at the age of 40 was actually my very first time to be "out on my own." It's something most of us do as teenagers when we go to college, or move out and work. Yet I had never faced those life lessons nor gone through that learning curve of what it means to be independent, self-reliant, self-focused and the person "in charge."

The more I feel I need whatever the answer to my prayer is, the harder it seems to be to have the faith to support that prayer.

Learning curves require just that: learning. And habits are hard to break. My twenty-two year habit of a full house was incredibly hard to break. Harder than I ever imagined it could be. My perceived felt-need for companionship made itself noticed in my mind and heart *all—the—time.* Yet having experienced a bitter divorce (what divorce isn't bitter?) coupled with decades of an empty marriage—a marriage literally forced as a young teen due to an unplanned pregnancy—my confidence in and desire for a dating relationship was very low. I had mixed requests inside of me. I needed what I had known—a presence in the home. Yet I also feared what I had known—what that presence might ultimately mean.

As a result, I put off dating entirely for several years after becoming single, only to give it my first try in year three—long distance, of course. Far enough to feel safe. As you might imagine, it didn't last long. A few months into it, I called it off. For no real reason, actually. He was (and still is) a great man. I just wasn't ready to date.

Another year passed and age continued to creep up on me while the house continued to loom empty. I had learned by then the simple tricks most people learn early on—how to fix things, call repairmen if you need to, how to fill a weekend, pay bills, and take vacations by myself. I had learned to go to movies alone, set a routine in the home, and I was learning to trust again. God had put a number of kind men in my life during that time through work and church. They modeled strength of character, love to their families, commitment to their wives and emotional stability. My fears were dissipating, thanks to them and thanks to time, but not entirely gone.

And my home was still empty.

What was the very worst part, though, if I am being completely, transparently, and vulnerably honest—I hadn't yet learned how to sleep well alone.

I'll admit—and I know this is personal—sleeping

alone was never my strength. Even as a child, I slept in my parents' room most nights. All the way into my teen years, I would wake up in the middle of the night, and, if my dad was away on business (he was an airline pilot), I would climb into my mom's big bed. If he was home, I would take my pillow and blanket and lay on the floor next to my mom's side of the bed. Yes, I slept on the floor a lot growing up.

Later, when I was married and my husband would travel, I would often end up on the floor of one of the kid's rooms. Or on the couch, close enough to hear them breathe. For whatever reason, I don't sleep well alone.

So this area—even after four years of being single, still created a nightly struggle and a daily dread. The first year after the divorce, a good friend would call every single night before going to sleep to help put my mind at rest. If there wasn't enough time to talk, I would still get the call with a routine phrase being said. It did help. It got me through that difficult first year of transition. But a phone call is not a person in the room and as the years grew, so did my desires for physical presence and proximity. These desires dominated my thoughts and emotions.

As this struggle only increased into year four, I begged God to introduce me to someone I could marry— someone I would feel comfortable with. Someone who would make me laugh. Someone I could love affectionately and also respect. My hopes weren't many, but I still didn't know where I would find that someone. So I gave my hopes to God and prayed.

After all, at my age, where do you meet someone anyhow? It's a true challenge for a lot of us who find ourselves single in mid-life. Work, church and kids take up most of life's time, and you're not likely to bump into any available suitors at the grocery store.

I knew my need but didn't know how to meet it. That's why I decided, through the encouragement of a close friend, and based on the promise in Philippians 4:19 that God will meet all our needs, to do a complete fast for seven days and ask God to provide me with my future mate. I had done a 21 day fast for the same thing the year before. Second time should be a charm. Plus, He is God, after all. This shouldn't be hard for Him to do. So I fasted, reminded Him repeatedly of His Word and asked Him to bring this person straight to me.

Funny enough, He did bring me a person.

On the sixth night of my seven-day fast, He did just that. As I walked out of the church sanctuary after a Wednesday night service, a man approached me to talk. I had seen him before but just in passing—it had been over eight months since we had last talked, and even then it had been brief. Yet something seemed different about him this night. Was he taller? More attractive? Older? I felt drawn to him somehow.

He would later joke I felt that way because I had gone without food for so long and that had obviously warped my vision and thoughts. Whatever it was, something drew me to him this time, unlike the times I had seen him before. Lo and behold, before I got into my car to leave that very night—on the sixth night of my fast, he asked me out.

Right then and there I believed God had answered my prayer. You go, God! Right? Well—we'll see.

We began dating that weekend and within weeks I had lost all my senses and fallen madly for this man. After all, why should I put up any guard? He was the answer to my prayer! He came to me while I was fasting for a mate. Surely he was *the one*.

"I have learned to move man through prayer alone."

True, he was the first man I had dated locally since becoming single. Or, ever even – as an adult. True, I had gotten married as a teenager so I could claim absolutely **no** experience in the ways and wiles of the heart in adult dating relationships. True, my co-workers told me I resembled an 8th grader in how I *ooh'd* and *aah'd* about him on and on and on (ad nauseam to them I'm sure). In fact, I felt like I was in the 8th grade all over again. This was my first real crush (i.e learning curve). But I thought it had to be real love. I walked around with a foolish smile plastered all over my face, barely able to pay attention at work. Yep, mature. As you might imagine, I spent every moment I could with this man of my so-called dreams— long days, even longer evenings. I was most definitely "in over my head."

Life moved along smoothly over the next several months, and I began to believe even more deeply that this would be the man I would one day marry. We never argued, and we laughed an awful lot. He never got angry, and I had no reason to fear that he would. I respected his mind and intelligence, and his voice enraptured me. What's best is that we enjoyed each other's company doing the most mundane things. It just felt right on a whole lot of levels. Did I mention he was hot? Yup.

But something happened several months into our relationship that came as a surprise. It was more of a storm. It happened all within a 24-hour period. And as quick as the relationship had formed, it had dissolved.

Suddenly.

His decision, not mine.

I was devastated, to say the least. My heart exploded into a million pieces. We had never even had a disagreement before. And now it was over? After three months? Just like that? I tried to contact him to see if we could talk it out, but he wouldn't return my calls. So I texted him. Occasionally he would text back something vague, but most times he didn't return texts either. Come to find out later, he had gone to an all-nighter in Oklahoma (if you know what that means). But I gave him the benefit of the doubt that it wouldn't happen again. So I kept reaching out. No, I didn't stalk him, but I'm sure I did break a number of "don't do" rules in *The Guide To Breaking Up Well.*

I was a hot mess.

I know. But he held my hopes, and I didn't want to let them go.

After a few weeks, I realized I couldn't continue like this. So I tried to focus my energy on something productive. I tried to follow everyone else's advice and just stay busy until the pain would go away. Surely the pain would go away. Right?

Another month passed, and I found myself invited to a special screening of an upcoming movie on the power of prayer in marriage and relationships called *War Room.* *War Room* has since gone on to become a major blockbuster hit and has changed lives throughout the world. But on that evening it was an unfinished film flickering on a television screen in a hotel room—without music at times and missing scenes. Even so, it was still just as powerful as the later big-screen debut.

While sitting in the back of that hotel suite in Nashville in a quaint gathering of a few of the cast members, family and producers, I immediately resonated with the main character throughout the whole film. After all, in the movie, they did not really highlight anything she had done wrong. The marriage was a disaster, but, as far as I could tell, it was all his fault. (When is it ever all one person's fault?) *Great, she's my hero*, I thought. Priscilla (the actress who played the main character) sat in front of me as we watched. It must be fate. A sign from God. *But, of course! This was my answer!*

I decided if praying had worked for the woman in the film to restore her relationship and get her man "back in line," than it would have to work for me too. I determined right then and there that I would "war room" my guy straight back into my arms (and simply overlook the red flag of the overnighter out of state).

So I got ready. Prepared my strategy. And chose to approach this war room like I did my work. It would be the best, most efficient, most thorough war room on the planet. I cleared a space in my closet, brought in mounds of books and all five of my beloved Bibles. I brought pens, paper and a prayer rug to kneel on. This would be where I would do my battles and win my war. And before you know it, the man of my so-called dreams would be mine again.

Granted, we had not communicated in over a month.

Didn't matter, though. I was convinced all I needed to do was go in my little war room prayer closet and pray. So I did. And, funny enough, within days Mr. Say-Nothing-At-All called me. Indeed. Out of the clear blue. So I acted surprised, of course, but I wasn't surprised at all. We began talking. He gave some excuse for what happened— said it wouldn't happen again—and told me he wanted us to try again. Play the music, I thought. Turn on the cameras. Cue the extras. We are starring in our own *War Room, Part Two*. Of course I forgave him immediately and things were resolved rather quickly. In fact, we picked things up just as if there had been no gap at all. *Yes!* Score one for Heather in her war room. I can do this!

In fact, score two for Heather because now things were even better than before. I knew I would marry this man. After all, he had showed up when I was fasting for a mate!

Granted—my family members, my pastor and my friends, by this point, were trying to tell me this was not the right direction for me. They were trying to point out how things had dissolved quite unnaturally, and under too sudden of a method. They pointed out the potential for that one-night becoming many. He didn't attend church regularly. Didn't pray. And they saw my music and movie choices devolve into things I wouldn't normally entertain. They knew this wasn't my dream – I was just tired of being alone. But no, I would hear none of it, of course. Even though they were all saying very similar things.

It didn't matter because they didn't realize how hard it was to be alone when you never had to be alone before. And besides—God had brought this man directly to me, hadn't He? On my fast. I had been fasting for a mate. And now God had even returned him through my war room efforts. This had to be fate. I ignored my naysayers. After all, what do they know?

Life went along pretty great after that for some time. I was a living example of the film, I thought. A poster child of its formulaic success. Take that, Satan - bam!

That is until that one day. Yea, that one day. We were having a really great time until something came up that concerned me. I tried not to let it bother me, but it did. I tried to ignore it, but I couldn't. I tried to explain it away, yet it lingered. I tried to play it down, but I couldn't. The day finished fine, but the next one came, and the thing that had happened—well, it was a huge red flag, take two. Because of how things had dissolved so quickly before, I ended things myself quickly on this go around so as to not have to worry whether it will end or not.

Have you ever done that? Afraid of losing something so you go ahead and lose it yourself – that way you won't have to live with the fear of losing it?

We call that self-protection but in all honestly it's just fear. Foolishness from fear. But I ended it nonetheless. Drastically. Decidedly. It was over, again.

Well I guess not so decidedly for me, after all. Because after a few days passed for me, I regretted the loss that came with the new vacuum. I wanted the space filled again. I wanted *us* back. I could overlook what I had seen.

Maybe I just wanted *an* "us" back, I don't know.

Big difference. Especially to God. Especially in prayer.

So amid internal mixed emotions and now limiting beliefs, I decided to "war room" him once again. It had worked the first time; surely it would work again.

I dug in.

I did all the same things I had done before, and then some. I fasted. I wrote out every untruth and lie I had allowed the enemy to plant in my mind regarding our relationship, and I countered it with God's Word. I bound those demons, loosed those angels and prayed the blood of Jesus Christ over everything. I repented of sins I should have repented of, and I repented of sins I hadn't even done. I was willing to do anything to get back this "us" – to fill this gap. A friend in Kenya got up at 3 a.m. for the two of us to spend 30 minutes in prayer together for clarification on this relationship. Other friends prayed for my clarification. One friend even fasted a meal a week specifically for clarification for this relationship. This friend didn't think I should seek to reconcile the relationship so he asked God to clarify it for me. I was so confused. My mind wanted him back but my heart was somehow unsure now.

Regardless of how much I did though by way of prayer and repentance, there was no movement on either side. We communicated, but neither of us felt like things should go back to the way they had been before. There was no happy ending like the previous time where God ushered in a remarkable reunion. It seemed, actually, to just get more distant the more I prayed.

I considered moving on and starting from scratch. Finding someone new. Starting again. So I tried that too. But sitting across a dinner table at a candlelit dinner with a man who was interested in dating me, all I could think of was that very process of starting from scratch.

I didn't want to start again. I didn't want to go through all of that time learning, building and bonding again with someone new. Only to possibly lose it again. I just wanted an *us* that would last. I wanted God to put an *us* back together again.

But He didn't.

Sure, we would get back together for an occasion here or there. A concert or a movie or a Saturday watching sports. But the relationship was never the same, and my limiting beliefs remained. In fact, even more of them came. And as they did, my prayers grew fewer and further between.

My war room became a closet once again.

Eventually, my prayers for this relationship ceased.

But as emotional and spiritual silence settled in, a question lingered in the hole it left behind: **Why was I able to pray this relationship back to full flame the first time, but I wasn't able to "war room" anything**

worthwhile on the second try? My approach had been the same. In fact, my prayers had even increased. My fasting had increased. The number of friends praying with me had also increased. So why didn't my war room work this time? Why, God, Why?

Yes, I asked Him more than once.

Why?

Why? *Why?*

I didn't get it. I didn't understand. Hours in prayer had produced nothing of substance or value the second time around. Why not? I struggled to understand how a process He asks us to do—the process of prayer—could work one time but not the next? God had definitely caught my attention with this situation of *twice*.

It was a good question. A question I couldn't ignore. A question I couldn't stuff under the blankets of my saddened soul. It kept begging to be answered. Yet I had no answer. I couldn't figure out why.

That's when I decided to set out on this journey to seek an answer. I sought an answer because that question mattered. In fact, that question made every difference in the world to me. I was baffled.

See, I'm a processes-girl. Anyone who has ever worked with me knows I'm a systems and processes-girl. But the question and problem I was facing in these two situations was that this particular "process" of prayer, if I were to be honest, seemed broken.

I don't like broken processes. Who does? They're inefficient. Untrustworthy. And cause more problems than they cure. That is why I couldn't ignore this question, no matter what seeking to answer it would cost me in terms of time, emotions or energy. I didn't care. I needed to find out.

So I threw myself into locating the answer for the

better part of the next three years. I must have read over 60 books, listened to countless hours of lectures and sermons, tried every approach and suggestion offered. I dug into belief systems and practices I hadn't even heard of before. I dug even deeper into my own tender soul. It didn't matter how much it hurt or what I found when I dug, I just kept going. If the exact same process had worked the first time, why didn't it work the next?

But the more I dug, the louder the question roared: Why didn't it work *twice*?

I had to find out what part of the process was off.

Was it God?

Was it me?

Was it the approach?

Was it the words I chose?

Was it my interpretation of God's teachings on prayer?

Was it my thoughts?

Was it complaining?

Was it the request itself?

Was it the frequency of my prayers?

Was it faith? Or a lack thereof?

And what exactly was in that mustard seed that moved my mountain the first time but wasn't able to on the second try?

What

      was

         wrong

            this

               time?

One of my heroes, 18th century missionary to China Hudson Taylor, once said, **"I have learned to move man through prayer alone."** His life reflected that truth.

I desperately wanted to learn that too.

No. I *needed* to learn that too.

We all do.

CHAPTER 3: TWO MORE BARNEY SHOWS

You and I are not alone when we ask these questions. We don't need to feel ashamed or hide the truth that hard, difficult questions like these exist. In fact, you and I are in good company to cry out to God and ask whether He has even heard us. The pages of His parchment contain person after person wondering where God is, why He's taking so long and whether or not He even cares.

David—the man after God's own heart—cried out time and time again. One of those times he even asked if God had forgotten about him altogether. Now, if God said that David had a heart like His, then He must have been a pretty spiritual man, right? David was someone to look up to and learn from. Yet David still prayed fairly harsh prayers,

"How long, O Lord, Will You forget me forever? How long will You hide Your face from me? How long shall I take counsel in my soul, *Having* sorrow in my heart all the day? How long will my enemy be exalted over me? Consider *and* answer me, O Lord my God..."

If you or I were to stand up and say something like that in a church Sunday School class, we might be politely asked to sit back down. After a few compassionate looks came our way, we would be reminded that God says to always "give thanks." Then we might be reminded that there are people worse off than we are. To think positive thoughts. To realize that God's ways are not our ways so we should accept them and move on. What good is questioning things anyhow? Be mindful—lightning might strike you if you speak too openly about stuff like that. (Okay, maybe the last one is a bit extreme). Or, maybe not?

But for whatever reasons, and I'm sure they are probably well-intentioned, we get nervous when people question God. We may even get nervous when we question Him ourselves.

But David did it. David asked for an answer. David wanted a solution. He needed God to be a better friend than He was being right then. He needed His help.

And so he asked God a pretty hurtful question, if you think about it. He asked if God had forgotten him altogether because the One he had always leaned on didn't seem to be there for him right then.

If you have ever felt that way, or anything similar, then take comfort that you are not the only one. Perhaps all that means is that you are a man or a woman after God's own heart as well. You are not the only one.

We are not the only ones who question where God is and what He is doing.

There was also the prophet Habakkuk who accused

God of not hearing him. This is a prophet, nonetheless, an appointed spokesman of God, writing these words,

> "How long, O Lord, will I call for help, And You will not hear? I cry out to You "Violence" but You do not save." (Habakkuk 1:2).

That's an accusation, not a question. Habakkuk accused God of not hearing him when he needed Him to hear him most.

And let's not forget about Job, the righteous man who said, "I cry out to You for help, but You do not answer me; I stand up, and You turn Your attention against me" (Job 30:20). That's not Job saying, "Are you listening, God?" That's Job saying, "You've turned your back on me. You've abandoned me to my problem all alone." Job wondered, as so many of us have wondered at one time or another, if God truly was good after all.

Then there's Joseph who was not only thrown in a pit, but also sold as a slave and wasted away in prison in a foreign land for years. Years. Yes, we read that the whole time God was "with Joseph," but I've often wondered if Joseph knew that God was with him. Or did Joseph want to know why life was taking so many difficult turns? I think he did. Especially because Joseph chose to complain when he asked the cupbearer to remember him when he got out of prison (Genesis 40:15). First, Joseph brought up the fact he had been kidnapped, then next that he was wrongfully jailed. This doesn't sound like the same Joseph who we hail as saying, "As for you, you meant evil for me but God meant it for good …."

In fact, I wonder if it was because of Joseph's complaining spirit (even more so what that spirit revealed - a still bitter, untrusting heart. Sound like self-pity, anyone?) that kept him stuck in that pit two years longer than he had to be. I think it did, similar to how our complaining keeps us in our pits far too long (even if that complaining is justified.)

And what about Moses? Did Moses ever wonder what had happened to God and to the hopes He had placed in his heart? Did he doubt God's loyalty during the 40 years he wandered the backside of the desert herding smelly, noisy, dirty sheep? He definitely seemed surprised to hear from God when He finally did show up in the burning bush.

We are not the only ones who question where God is and what He is doing.

Or what about Martha and Mary who watched their beloved brother die all the while knowing that Jesus could have saved him? Did Martha regret cooking for Him so frequently? Did Mary feel betrayed for having made what, at the time, was called the better choice in sitting at His feet? Did she wonder where that "better choice" had actually gotten her in the end? Did they both question Jesus' level of honesty, compassion and commitment?

Or what about another prophet, Jeremiah? I stumbled across this passage one day while sitting perplexed in my prayer closet complaining to God that He was being so mean by allowing this issue to drag on for so long. I was simply tired of it all. Yes, I felt feelings of guilt for how upset my heart was toward God. This was the God of the universe, after all. And yes, I said some pretty not-very-nice things about Him to a close friend, and also to Him directly. I definitely felt less-than-spiritual, which is not a great way to feel while actually in your prayer closet.

When you feel guilty or less-than-spiritual, you begin to question whether or not you should even pray at all. If you've made God mad, then why would He want to listen? Do you even have a right to approach Him, to go to His throne, let alone **boldly**? (Hebrews 4:16) Sometimes you may not feel like you do. At least I didn't right about then.

Did Martha wonder where that "better choice" had actually gotten her in the end?

So I was stuck. I sat there stuck in my upset feelings knowing that I needed to go to the only One who could help me but doubting whether He really wanted to hear from me. I think Satan may delight in keeping us stuck in thoughts like so we won't pray when we need to the most. That's right where he had me.

I didn't know if I should pray or if it would just be a waste of time. I didn't know if I should allow myself to become emotionally vulnerable with God only to have Him give me the cold shoulder because of some of the things I had just said about Him. My guilt put me on pause so I decided to do what I often do when I don't know what to do—and that's a Bible-flip.

A Bible-flip is where I pray for help, guidance, insight, comfort, assurance—whatever it is at the moment—and then flip open my Bible and read what God says. It's not anything taught in Bible study methods class, I assure you, but it is a simple habit I picked up decades ago. And, for me at least, it seems to work. So I prayed. I flipped. And this time I opened my Bible right to the book of Jeremiah, chapter 15. My eyes immediately landed on verse 18, which is Jeremiah speaking.

The prophet cries out,

"Why has my pain been perpetual, And my wound incurable, refusing to be healed? Will You indeed be to me like a deceptive *stream*. With water that is unreliable?"

I read and re-read the words again and again to make sure I had seen them right. But that's exactly what it said, I promise you. You can read it yourself.

As the words sunk it, I began to thank God for showing them to me. I realized I'm not the only one who feels like He has somehow hoodwinked me. Jeremiah himself said God was acting like a deceptive stream. He felt like God had set him up, lied to him. He felt tricked and he wasn't afraid to admit it.

"Will You indeed be to me like a deceptive stream. With water that is unreliable?"

Reading that passage immediately set my heart at ease. If a prophet could go so far in his thinking and questions as that, then I was fairly certain God could handle me. It was as if God was using that verse to assure my soul that He has pretty thick skin after all. Go ahead and pray, I felt. He can take it. He can look past my rocky emotions—even when they have bubbled over into accusations, doubts, questions and more. God understands that I am human.

And my friend, guess what—He understands that you are human too. Psalm 103:14 tells us, "For He Himself knows our frame; He is mindful that we are but dust."

He knows we are finite beings viewing our world through a perception cloaked in five physical senses, and an understanding often confined to what we have personally experienced. I have a hunch God may judge us a lot lighter than we often judge ourselves. This is because He remembers what we often forget—how He made us from the dirt of the ground. He knows we are on a spiritual path that can often elude our physical capacity for comprehension.

God understands that you are human too.

To question whether or not God is listening or even whether or not He cares is not a sign of an evil soul. It is a sign that you and I are *human*. And just like the prophet who asked God, "How long?" and just like the man after God's own heart who asked Him, "How long?" and just like Mary and Martha who stood on the side of their road straining their eyes for Jesus, and wondering, "How long?"—you and I are free to do the same.

"How long, oh God? Are You even listening to me?" *It's okay to ask.*

God Chooses How To Answer

But remember—when we do ask, He is also free to

answer as He chooses. Sometimes He will answer with a merciful grace in a way we can understand. Similar to when you are taking a family road trip on vacation and the kids keep asking, "How long? How long? How long?" You try to answer in a way they will understand.

When my kids were younger and this would happen, I would always try to put it in a way they could grasp. Because to say, "We'll be there in 130 miles," wouldn't mean anything to them. Or even, "We have to go through Nairobi traffic and then it should be another two hours." None of that would mean a thing. So I would put our trips in Barney shows. "We'll be there in 2 Barney shows," I would say, if we had another hour to go—changing the number based on how far was left.

At times, God will be gracious to do that with us. He'll let us get a glimpse of the end of our trial, struggle or wait. But other times, like Jesus delaying His trip to raise Lazarus, He chooses to answer with an ongoing wait.

He'll leave us hanging.

To question whether or not God is listening or even whether or not He cares is not a sign of an evil soul. It is a sign that you and I are human.

And then there are even those times He may even rebuke us like He often did His disciples. And when He does, we need to listen and accept it. He is God. It is His choice. He knows what is best at that very moment in our lives. So when we ask, we must be prepared for His answer. God does not often mince His words, and ultimately the problem with our prayers is never about

Him, the problem is always within us. Yet what makes that problem all the more a problem is that it is usually ever-changing.

In fact, there are many reasons why our prayers get no reply. That's one of the first lessons I began to spot on this personal prayer search. The reasons are legion, and they can vary.

Because there are so many reasons, we would do well to never seek to lock God into a box and demand that He always operate or respond a certain way. Each prayer need—each scenario we face—requires us to look through the various reasons why prayers go unresolved and then aim to address them. A reason that showed up in one situation may not be the same reason for the next.

Similar to how David sought God and His wisdom and strategy for each and every battle he faced, we are to do the same.[2] David knew he couldn't take the identical approach into every city he set out to conquer. If he did, he would lose more times than not.

Neither can we.

Every battle, every problem, every prayer request we have requires individual attention, introspection and revelation. The Christian life is an *every-day* experience. It's not a "push play and go." When we get too lazy (ahem...I mean—busy) to engage God every single day in every single pursuit and opt rather for applying the same formula to each separate thing, we will find our prayers bouncing off of the walls of our war room rather than penetrating through them.

Prayer isn't a process we master one day and then use

---

[2] See 1 Samuel 23:1-3, 1 Samuel 23:4-5, 1 Samuel 23:10-11, 1 Samuel 23:12-14, 1 Samuel 30:8-9, 2 Samuel 2:1-2, 2 Samuel 5:17-21, 2 Samuel 5:22-25, 2 Samuel 21:1.

on rinse & repeat.

What worked for one situation will most likely *not* work for the next. Ask David about his battles. He had to constantly change his plan. Your prayer closet list or notes posted to your refrigerator may prove successful in one scenario but not in another. Your prayerful journaling or free-writing may work well for one need in providing you with direction but not in another. That binding and loosing of demons and angels may work great for one situation but not for another.

For example, persistent begging and pleading worked well for one problem (consider the neighbor at the door banging again and again in Luke 11:5-8) while a simple word of gratitude worked for another (consider Jesus feeding five thousand in John 6:11).

In both of those situations, the people needed the exact same thing. They sought the exact same outcome. They both needed bread. But both of them took a very different approach to getting it.

And guess what—both got their bread.

To say, teach, instruct, or claim that there is one sure-way to get your prayers answered is naïve. The Bible doesn't do that, outside of an abiding and pure faith. But the dynamics of that abiding faith will differ in as many ways as our emotions can as well. In fact, the construct and content of our faith will vary based on the situation. The substance of Peter's faith when he told the lame man to walk outside of the gate called Beautiful was a very different substance than the faith (or lack of faith) he had when he tried to walk on water (Acts 3:6, Matthew 14:29).

The action he was seeking was the same in both situations—walking. But the faith he brought to his prayer was not the same at all.

> *Every battle, every problem, every prayer request we have requires individual attention, introspection and revelation. The Christian life is an every-day experience.*

Like Peter, our faith is fluid depending on what we are facing. We are not robots. Our desires mold into new shapes as we move forward through our hours and our days. Our hearts, beliefs, limiting beliefs and mindsets are continually evolving. We are never in the exact same space of who we are for more than a moment. We are constantly learning, un-learning, absorbing and shifting within ourselves—within our soul, within our spirit.

Likewise, our issues are multi-dimensional as well. They are complex and ever-changing.

Because of this, prayer—and our approach both *to* it and *in* it—must be adaptable as well.

Productive prayer often requires an abiding and variable communion with the very heart of God. Prayer becomes more about understanding ourselves honestly while also connecting *with* God authentically. Rather than simply speaking *to* Him ritually.

Jesus gave us the greatest insight into effective prayer when He spoke with the woman at the well. He wasn't speaking about prayer but the reality He touched on applied nonetheless.

He told her,

"God is spirit, and those who worship Him must worship in spirit and truth," (John 4:24).

When you and I come to God in prayer, we must come in spirit *and* in truth. What's more, it must be God's truth and not the truth we so often set up as worldviews or cultural persuasions for ourselves. God's truth is the only real truth just like two plus two will always and only equal four. No matter what we say. No matter what we want our truth to be. God's truth is truth, period.

Prayer isn't a process we master one day and then use on rinse and repeat. What worked for one situation will most likely not work for the next.

One of the most critical truths in God's economy is that of His holiness. That's why I chose this common block to answered prayer as our starting point to more fully answering our questions on prayer. God's holiness is an undeniable and unchangeable aspect of who He is. Due to His holiness, He has standards, whether we like them or not. These standards affect our prayers. If you find this particular reason for blocked prayer resonating with you (as you read on) or your situation, simply acknowledge it, make the adjustments where you need to, and re-approach your request from there.

A Common Block to Answered Prayer

Toe-stepping time. Mine too. But, we must—so let's do this. One of the most common blocks to answered prayer is... yep, sin. Sorry to go here, but we need to.

As I just mentioned, God is holy. He is a pure radiance of light. When we harbor darkness and impurity in our hearts, it naturally causes a separation between us and Him. Just as you wouldn't be able to hear me if I was standing in Maine and you in California —no matter how loud I shouted—separation always leads to a lack of effectiveness in communication.

Sin isn't something we like to talk about, though. I don't think it's something we even like to think about. Yet when we fail to acknowledge and address it, it can show up as a block in our prayer life. That's why one of the very first things we need to do when we stumble upon unanswered prayers is to consider Isaiah 59:1-2.

> "Behold, the Lord's hand is not so short that it cannot save; Nor is His ear so dull that it cannot hear. But your iniquities have made a separation between you and your God, and your sins have hidden His face from you so that He does not hear."

Psalm 66:18 puts it this way, "If I regard wickedness in my heart, The Lord will not hear."

That's plain, simple and straightforward truth. If you, or I, regard sin in our hearts—*God does not hear.*

Ouch, right?

Because of this truth, when we struggle in prayer we need to consider whether there is hidden or unconfessed sin in our lives. Now, that doesn't mean we have to be perfect to get our prayers answered. As Solomon penned, "Indeed, there is not a righteous man on earth who *continually* does good and who never sins," (Ecclesiastes 7:20). No one is without sin. No human is perfect. But what it does mean is that we need to be honest with God and ourselves about our sin and struggles, confessing what we know is wrong and asking Him to reveal what we don't.

Keep in mind, not all sin falls into what we often consider as the *biggies* in sin. Stealing, sexual immorality, swearing, getting drunk, porn—these are ones we frequently go to first when we consider our sin checklist. And while they are bad and grievous sins, what we fail to realize is that oftentimes throughout Scripture, God was far more concerned with and burdened by sins of the heart (i.e. pride, jealousy, selfish ambition, greed, apathy, bitterness, materialism, and more) than sins of the flesh.

One thing that struck me in my late 20s as I was reading through the Old Testament was a passage I came upon in Ezekiel. This passage literally screamed from the page, begging for my attention. Prior to reading it, I had always thought that Sodom and Gomorrah had gotten destroyed due to homosexuality. Maybe you have a similar thought. But when I read this passage, I saw otherwise. Reading it over and over, I sat there stunned. I sat there amazed.

I sat there *guilty*.

It was the sin of apathy and selfishness which provoked God's anger to destroy those infamous two towns. The citizens of Sodom and Gomorrah had become proud in their abundance. In their pride, they also ignored the plight of those less fortunate than them who lived in the fringes of their land. We read,

> "Behold, this was the guilt of your sister Sodom: she and her daughters had arrogance, abundant food and careless ease, but she did not help the poor and needy. Thus they were haughty and committed abominations before Me. Therefore I removed them when I saw it," (Ezekiel 16:49-50).

Arrogance and self-serving decisions stirred the anger in God's heart. It was an issue of injustice that incensed God and ushered in their demise. Things like social, racial and class disparity grieve God severely. That makes sense because we are all made in His image. To Him, we are equal no matter who we are (Galatians 3:28).

So important are these issues that Jesus spent nearly a fifth of His recorded teaching time focused on the area of money and possessions. That's more than what He taught on heaven and hell combined. Over 300 verses in the Bible specifically cover the area of poverty and social injustice. That's almost the same number of verses on the subject of faith.

Materialism and selfishness, to the exclusion of helping others, is an affront to God's core values. Yet it is not a subject we hear preached on in our churches or taught over our radio and television broadcasts very often, if at all. At best, we are indifferent to the needs of the poor and disadvantaged in our nation and around the world. At worst, we are callous—even heartless.

Some sins seem obvious to us, yes. But other sins hover hidden in our blind-spots. Yet it's the hidden ones that will often bite us. These are the sins we don't always realize we are doing and far too often overlook in our own lives. That's why personal discipleship is such an important aspect of living a life of authoritative prayer. It's also why self-awareness and honesty are so crucial, as well as accountability from well-meaning friends.

Another reason that these types of sin are easy to miss is because our culture promotes personal gain, comfort, progress and indulgence—even our Christian culture promotes this to a large degree. We are often taught the very opposite of the virtues of charity, prudence and temperance. Yet it is things like charity, prudence and temperance which please the heart of God and open His ears to our own cry.

A third reason why they are easy to overlook is because they are typically things we *don't* do as compared to things we *do*. These offenses go by the name of "sins of omission" because the word omission refers to *not* doing something. This is compared to "sins of commission" (something we actually do that is wrong).

James writes boldly and clearly regarding sins of omission:

"Therefore, to one who knows the right thing to do and does not do it, to him it is sin," (James 4:17).

God speaks brashly about the impact of these sins on our prayer lives,

"He who shuts his ear to the cry of the poor will also cry himself and not be answered," (Proverbs 21:13).

As we continue to witness Christian lives devolve, prayer lives become anemic and our collective societal impact fade, these are the sins we need to consider more fully and talk about more openly.

God really did say that when we ignore the plight of others in need, we literally sabotage our own prayer life. That's not something we learn in Sunday School, or in our movies.

But that's Biblical. And that's deep.

Read Proverbs 21:13 again. "He who shuts his ear to the cry of the poor will also cry himself and not be answered." Let that sink in.

---

*God really did say that when we
ignore the plight of others in need,
we literally sabotage our
own prayer life.*

Sin in Someone Else's Life

But not only do our own sins hinder our own prayers, but unfortunately because we live in a sinful world—we are impacted by other people's sins as well. For example, if a spouse wants a divorce while the other spouse is asking for a time to focus on reconciliation, that spouse's prayers for restoration may not be answered. Or if a divorced spouse wants to reconcile but their ex is already remarried, that will negatively impact that prayer as well.

God will never impose His will on someone else and force them to comply with what is right. It's called free will. If the other person has a heart that is hardened, God will not force reconciliation.

A few years ago when I was still single, I experienced something on a more minor level but still a rather sticky situation with a man who had been trying to date me for a period of time. He was a successful business man I had met through work. He had a private pilot's license and a history with similar experiences of overseas living in common with me. He was a nice man from what I could tell. An adventure-seeker, which balances out my more non-risky routines. He was an A-level executive for a Fortune 100 company and had shared with me that he was divorced and wanted to date me. I never quite felt right about it so I continued to put him off. Ultimately after nine months of asking, I gave in and said I'd go out. The day of the date came and I still didn't feel good about it. But I had no real reason to keep putting this man off. He had been persistent and kind.

> "He who shuts his ear to the cry of the poor will also cry himself and not be answered."

I had mentioned to a couple of my friends as well as my daughter that I was not looking forward to the date at all. The morning of the date came. I woke up and went about my normal business. My daughter had been encouraging me to take a round of probiotics since she had recently gotten on a health-kick. I was in a hurry with several meetings, a taping and the date that night so I took my probiotic with a glass of water—skipped breakfast—and proceeded to get dressed.

About 10 minutes later I was kneeled-over and up-chucking in the bathroom. My daughter came in to see what was wrong and neither of us made the connection to the probiotic on an empty stomach so we assumed I had the flu. Thus, I called in sick to work and cancelled the date.

I never did feel sick the rest of the day. Neither was I disappointed about missing the date since I hadn't been looking forward to it. It actually felt like a relief. But a few weeks later, I felt bad about not feeling ... well, *bad*. I thought maybe this is the man God has for me and I'm just being too picky (a not-so-great habit of mine).

So I decided to pray and ask God to open my eyes to see if this was the man He had for me, and to bring us together if it was His will.

Lo and behold, about an hour later, I randomly ran across a post on Facebook from this man's... yep, his *wife*. You read that correctly. His *wife* tagged a photo of them together on his page with a "Happy 21st Anniversary" message. They were smiling. I was floored. And my probiotic-puking catastrophe made all the more sense now. God had spared me from a terrible disaster. This man had lied to me.

I had also gotten the answer to my prayer about whether this was someone God was connecting me with to date. And, no, He was not about to "bring us together" due to this man's obvious sin.

That's just one example of how we cannot control what other people choose to do. Yet what they do can often affect us and our prayers.

The Bible states clearly that a husband's sin toward his wife damages his prayers. As the spiritual head of the home, this no doubt trickles down to the wife and children through effects we probably rarely attribute correctly. 1 Peter 3:7 says,

"You husbands in the same way, live with your wives in an understanding way, as with someone weaker, since she is a woman; and show her honor as a fellow heir of the grace of life, so that your prayers will not be hindered."

When a husband fails to treat his wife the way the Lord desires him to do so, his prayers will be hindered. It is possible that the wife's prayers for their relationship and their mutual goals may be hindered as well, without her being aware as to why, until his sin is addressed. And if his sin goes unaddressed, that marriage may not make it

– despite all attempts to keep it together. Sin is a destroyer of relationships. It is also a hindrance to prayer. Whether it's our own sin or someone else's—it will damage the power of our prayers.

A Sin-Free Life. *Really?*

So what is the solution? Is it possible to live a sin-free life? No, I don't think so. Isaiah writes that even the good things we do are, at best, filthy rags, "All of us have become like one who is unclean, and all our righteous acts are like filthy rags; we all shrivel up like a leaf, and like the wind our sins sweep us away," (Isaiah 64:6, NIV).

I don't know about you but I've never been able to come close to being perfect for even a minute. Thoughts of worry, regret, fear, selfishness, laziness—you name it—they creep in regularly without me knocking them down, ultimately producing sin in my own thoughts, words, emotions or actions.

> *Whether it's our own sin or someone else's—sin will damage the effectiveness of our prayers.*

But for whatever reason, I've always been graced with a woeful awareness of my own sinfulness. Oh, joy! All kidding aside, I say "graced" because I have found it to be a blessing in disguise. One of the things I adore about the raw and purely abandoned faith of the earlier-century theologians like St. Francis of Assisi, St. John of the Cross and Augustine was their awareness of humanity's fallenness. They were so much more honest about our own depravity than it seems like we are today.

Being aware of our sinfulness is a good thing. It keeps us in alignment with the truth of who God is and who we are. It ought not to produce a dominance of shame as much as it should evoke a heart of gratitude. This is gratitude for God's mercy, His grace and His unmerited, undeserved favor. God is so holy and we are so sinful that nothing good He ever gives us is deserved.

My favorite Bible story by far and forever will be is the one of the publican (also referred to as a tax collector in some translations). You may know it but it's worth revisiting. It reads,

> "Two men went up into the temple to pray, one a Pharisee and the other a tax collector. The Pharisee stood and was praying this to himself: 'God, I thank You that I am not like other people: swindlers, unjust, adulterers, or even like this tax collector. I fast twice a week; I pay tithes of all that I get.' But the tax collector, standing some distance away, was even unwilling to lift up his eyes to heaven, but was beating his breast, saying, 'God, be merciful to me, the sinner!' I tell you, this man went to his house justified rather than the other; for everyone who exalts himself will be humbled, but he who humbles himself will be exalted." (Luke 18:10-14)

This was a story told by Jesus Himself. It is a graphically revealing story about the heart of God. At the end of the day, God is not impressed with our fasting, giving, meditating or doing—when it's done with a spirit of self-righteousness, entitlement or pride. God is most impressed with the broken heart of humility. As the 19th century spiritualist Andrew Murray has written,

"We will learn that we can never have more of true faith than we have of true humility."

Humility is that delicate virtue that allows us to do good things for God from a heart of duty (Luke 17:10) while simultaneously expecting favor from God in a heart of trust (James 4:6). Humility is the antidote to sin's negative effects in our lives and primarily in our prayers. Humility alone will break down the barrier and blockage sin erects in our prayer lives. It will not only capture God's heart, but it will also incline His ear to hear.

An authentic awareness and humility about our sins will get us on the path to more answered prayers. So will an increase in our desire to serve the Lord by helping others in need.

Yet that is only one step. It is only one portion of a battle plan. There will be times when your prayers are not answered, and it will have nothing to do with sin or pride or self-reliance or selfishness at all. Battles are complex. As is war. And on this field of spiritual warfare in this component we call prayer, there remain many other strategies to both employ and apply as we seek to reach our hearts into heaven and bring answers into our lives.

Humility will not only capture God's heart, but it will also incline His ear to hear.

Confession of sin is one. Humility before God is another. Asking with right motives is another. Or ridding yourself of double-mindedness.

And sometimes, the greatest hindrance to prayer is simply not asking at all.

But this next one we are going to look at is one we will dive into a bit more deeply in these pages because it is one that if gotten right, can have a lasting impact not only in our prayers but also in our peace while we wait for answered prayer.

And peace really does matter, doesn't it my friend?

The older I get, the more valuable I consider it to be. I imagine you do too.

CHAPTER 4: IF ONLY HEAVEN IS HAPPY

A private audience with the Pope. Or so it felt. Having waited over an hour for the line of earnest well-wishers and askers-of-questions to dwindle down for the guest speaker that night, it was finally my turn. I didn't mind waiting. After all, he was a man I had grown to respect greatly—as many millions do. I had spoken with him by phone on occasion before and had the opportunity to meet with him privately the previous year as well, but that was more concerning business. This time I had requested the meeting for a personal concern.

I had a question about prayer.

And if anyone were to know anything about prayer, the man whose pen had written the worldwide phenomenon on the subject (with over 10 million copies sold) would be the person to ask. The author of *The Prayer of Jabez*, no less.

As the last person with the last question walked off, the security guard ushered myself and Dr. Bruce Wilkinson back to the green room. He had preached his heart out at the evening revival service and then stood graciously by while person after person approached him with either something to share or something to ask. He looked tired, walked slowly and when we finally entered the room, made a dash for the water bottles and juice.

"Would you like a juice, too?" he asked, as humble in person as he seemed on stage.

"No, I'm okay," I said, wanting to get to my question. He sat down, drank the entire bottle of juice in one go and then smiled. We began by exchanging pleasantries, and then I proceeded to update him on where we were as an organization and how we had grown exponentially, once again, over the previous year. Dr. Bruce smiled and laughed in that characteristically bigger-than-life manner. He then settled in for the more personal discussion.

"That is all great," he said, "but I have a question…."

"Yes," I nodded, "Go ahead."

"Are you bored?"

Now it was my turn to laugh, more from nervousness than humor. I had my hands in multiple pockets, my plates piled with multiple projects, wearing more hats than Dr. Seuss's Bartholomew Cubbins himself. I had held the equivalent of two full-time jobs for five years and had recently added consulting on the side—what kind of question was that? And what kind of person would even think to ask it? But this was Dr. Bruce, a man known for being anything but conventional.

"Interesting you ask," I replied. "Because—I actually have found myself bored more often than not." I paused, wondering if I should continue. Should I feel guilty for admitting that? I have wonderful, rewarding jobs with wonderful, admirable people. Shouldn't I just be grateful? Yet I wanted his wisdom so I remained transparent. I decided to continue, "To be frank, I have actually been bored for about an entire year now."

He smiled his knowing grin.

"It's not for a lack of things to do," I stammered. "In fact, I don't know why it is—things are going great. We're growing, and I'm always busy with something new… But, for whatever reason, I admit—I get bored, more than I think I should."

Entrepreneurial himself—after all, this is the man who owns a 2500 acre ministry-based game park in South Africa, taught America how to "walk thru the Bible" from start to finish for decades, planted millions of gardens for the poor overseas, has sold over 20 million books… I knew he might understand the spirit of what I had just acknowledged. It isn't always the amount or scope of what you do that keeps boredom at bay. Rather, boredom is often an indicator of something deeper. Something more at the core. Maybe it's a passion that has been lost or a goal that has been accomplished. It can be any number of things.

"So…," he paused, apparently not wanting to allow this one to rest. He asked again, "You *are* bored?"

I nodded, "Yes, I am."

"Let me ask you another question then," he said, leaning toward me in his compassionate style.

"Absolutely," I replied, maintaining his gaze.

"Have you gotten married in the last year?"

I admit that question caught me by surprise. From business to boredom to marriage. What? I didn't quite follow the flow. Now, Dr. Bruce is known near and far as probably one of the most insightful ministers on the planet. His ability to discern heart issues in people's lives—even strangers—surpasses most. I sat there amazed, intrigued, alarmed and embarrassed—all at the same time.

"In fact," I said, my voice getting softer, "I have not."

He nodded, as if he knew.

"Oddly enough," I continued, "that's exactly why I had requested this meeting with you. I haven't gotten married in the past year—or even in the past many years—despite a deep desire to do so. Despite over a month of fasting from food to do so. Despite countless hours of prayer to do so," I paused again, looking down—wanting to make sure it was still fine to continue. He smiled. So I did, "That's what I wanted to ask you about."

Dr. Bruce relaxed, leaned back on the couch—his pastoral face revealing a look that said, "Ask. I've been here before."

So I went ahead.

"Why, sir," I began, "do my prayers on so many other things get answered so quickly—almost effortlessly even, yet my prayers for a mate continue to go unheard—unresolved, for so long. Or at least that's how it seems to me."

"Have you surrendered?" he asked.

"What do you mean?" I replied, taken aback at a word like that.

"Have you surrendered your desire for a husband to God?"

"I don't know," I answered. "What does that look like?"

He smiled, sat up a bit and opened with a reticent tone. He then proceeded with something to the sort of, "Well, I don't always talk about myself, but in answer to your question, I need to."

I was listening. All ears.

That's when he began to share about a time he had been asked to speak to one of the largest gatherings of men in a Promise Keepers event in Detroit, Michigan. Nearly 100,000 men filled the stadium, and they had asked Dr. Bruce to talk on a delicate subject: sexual purity. It was a talk he had given before, but this time was going to be different. Because this time, God had placed it on his heart to give an altar call for the men to come forward who needed to repent of immorality.

"You want me to do what?" Dr. Bruce asked, relaying to me his astonishment at what God was requesting him to do. "What if they don't want to come forward?" he continued. "What if no one comes forward at all?"

He then proceeded to explain how he told God he would look like a fool standing up there giving an altar call with no one moving around. This was the grand stage of Promise Keepers. His job as a speaker was to inspire, motivate, disciple and encourage. Not necessarily to ask everyone who might be doing something incredibly personally immoral to come forward in front of their pastor, their friends—possibly even their family—and confess it.

Maybe God had gotten this one wrong.

"Have you surrendered?" he asked.

Fear gripped Dr. Bruce so greatly he told me that he sought out an empty corner in the speaker's tent. He had gone to the speaker's tent on the side of the platform before he was to go up and talk. In this tent and in the corner by himself, he told me how he had knelt down with his stomach literally sick from nerves, explaining to God that he didn't really think he would be able to do what He was asking him to do.

Still a young man at that time—maybe 40 years old at best, faced with the largest audience he had yet to speak to, he was understandably nervous. My goodness, who could blame him? This was his moment on a national platform to rouse the stadium, not shut it down. God was asking him that rather than end on a note of grand inspiration evoking a standing crowd to end instead with a solemn humility and ask for repentance in one of the most private areas of sin.

What?

Are you serious?

That might not go over too well. Maybe they wouldn't even ask him back to speak again.

Dr. Bruce considered all of these things. He said it tore him up inside. But then he made a decision. In his bowed state, still in the tent, he prayed along these lines,

"Lord, I cannot go up there and do what I want to do and make myself and many people happy and, *at the same time,* go up there and do what You want me to do and make heaven happy. I can't do both. Because they contradict each other. It has to be one or the other this time because we don't agree.

So, Lord, *I surrender.* I will go up there and preach what You have put on my heart to preach. I will call the men to come forward in repentance just like You said. And if no one comes, then that's okay. If I look like a fool, then that's okay. Because I choose to surrender. If only heaven is happy at the end of tonight, heaven is enough for me."

"Did you do it?" I asked, assured the answer was yes.

"I did," he said, a smile breaking over his face.

"And what happened?" I wondered, curious as to the

outcome.

"They came forward to repent in the masses," he replied, clapping his hands together in that confident way he does. He then paused, choosing his words. And continued, "But even if they hadn't, Heather, heaven would have been happy. And that was enough for me. That's surrender."

I leaned back in my chair this time, took a deep breath and considered the wisdom of what I had just heard. Time passed. Thoughts raced. Dr. Bruce then broke the silence with a question, "If you never get married again, will you be okay with that?"

"Okay?" I repeated, for clarity. What does "okay" mean, anyhow?

"Yes, listen to my exact words," he said. "If you never marry again, will you be *okay* with that?"

I took some time to think about his question and then answered honestly, "No, sir. I would not be okay with that."

"Then you have not surrendered," Dr. Bruce replied, matter-of-factly.

"If only heaven is happy at the end of tonight, heaven is enough for me."

The air seemed to smother our thoughts with the silence. I really had nothing else to say. I could not force myself to surrender something I believed I literally needed. I am … *um*, wired as an affectionate person and – well, singlehood doesn't lend itself to that in any capacity at all. Doesn't God know that? He made me so I thought He should. But rather than share those details between just the two of us that night, I decided to stay quiet.

Dr. Bruce broke the silence again, "Early on in my ministry," he said, "I spent an entire night wrestling with God as a young man in prayer." He then went on to describe the evening. Where he was. How it took place. The anguish. The doubt. The struggle.

He continued, "Ultimately God asked me if He took away my voice and my ability to speak, would I be okay with that?"

"What did you say?" I asked, knowing this was one of the greatest orators of our time.

"I said, 'Yes, I'm okay with that.'"

"And you meant it?" I asked again.

"Yes," he said, "I meant it. God knew that I meant it. That's surrender."

He went on to explain that surrender always involves three critical components—your mind, your will and your heart. It is only surrender when all three agree. Sometimes surrender can come in the form of an action. Other times it comes as a simple acknowledgment of the soul. However it presents itself, God knows when we have truly surrendered in all three areas.

We spent some more time talking. He was very generous as I'm sure it had been a long day, and I was truly blessed through the wisdom of this man whom God has used and continues to use to touch and transform so many millions of lives. But as I walked to my car late that evening and made the long drive home from church, I knew I had received my personal answer to this particular prayer as to why God did not seem to reply, nor resolve it. It was simple. I had not truly surrendered the outcome to trusting that He knows best.

I would accept a "yes" or a "wait" from God. But I was in no mindset to accept a "no."

And that is *not* surrender.

As Holocaust-survivor Corrie Ten Boom has said,

"Hold everything in your hands lightly otherwise it hurts when God pries your fingers open." That's *surrender.*

As Elizabeth Elliott, widow to the martyred missionary Jim Elliot, has said,

"God never withholds from His child that which His love and wisdom call good. God's refusals are always merciful—"severe mercies" at times but mercies all the same. God never denies us our heart's desire except to give us something better... I realized that the deepest spiritual lessons are not learned by His letting us have our way in the end, but by His making us wait, bearing with us in love and patience until we are able to honestly pray what He taught His disciples to pray: Thy will be done." That's *surrender.*

> *Surrender always involves three critical components—your mind, your will and your heart. It is only surrender when all three agree.*

As one of my favorite spiritualists, Andrew Murray, has said,

"God cannot hear the prayers on our lips often because the desires of our heart after the world cry out to Him much more strongly and loudly than our desires for Him." *Surrender.*

Dr. Bruce's words haunted me over the next few days. They haunted me over the next few months. "Would you be okay, Heather, if only heaven was happy? Because that's surrender."

No, I thought again and again, I would not be okay. Not with this.

I had given up a lot for God over the course of my life, He knew that. I had put Him first a lot, from a very young age. Lord knows I had worked very hard for Him day upon day, night upon night—when no one was looking. I had been a stay-at-home mom, a missionary in Africa. And in the last decade as a Christian ghost-writer, I had racked up a stack nearly floor to ceiling of books, bible studies, devotionals – even prayer guides – with circulations totaling in the millions. Late nights. Holidays. Early mornings. Nearly zero social life. It had all been for

Him.

So no, to give up the one thing I thought I desired most, when I wasn't one to desire for much—no, I was not okay with that. No, not at all.

This was no fleeting thing. This was no casual request. I wanted a loving husband. Full-stop.

But apparently, because of that and more, my prayer got no reply. My prayer got no resolution. By resolution, I mean God didn't give me what I wanted, give me peace in the waiting, or remove the desire.

Why not?

Because I held too tightly to its outcome. Because I could not, would not, let it go. Anytime you set an idol (a desire, wish, need, person, whatever) on your heart's throne above God, you can probably expect His response to be: *Surrender.*

But how do we lay down our "Isaacs" as Abraham had to when God asked him to give up the son he loved most (Genesis 22).

How do we let go of what we believe to be the fulfillment of our deepest desire?

How do you force your emotions to do something they simply can't on their own?

Remember, Dr. Bruce explained how surrender is not just a decision of the mind. It involves the mind, the will and the heart. I could tell my mind all day long that I want to surrender, but that wouldn't change how I felt inside. That wouldn't eliminate resentment, regret, bitterness or even apathy toward God that comes when desires are not met.

You can't just say that you surrender and have God believe you. He's smarter than that. You have to mean it. But how can you mean something you don't want to?

How do you truly let go of what you don't want to?

Anytime you set an idol (a desire, wish, need, person, whatever) on your heart's throne above God, you can probably expect His response to be: Surrender.

Oprah once shared how as a young, unknown television personality she had quickly become obsessed with the book "The Color Purple." She ate, drank, breathed and lived this story.

She bought copies for all of her friends and pleaded with God to cast her in the film when she heard they were creating one.

Interestingly enough, she did get to audition for the film. But when weeks went by, and even months, she had heard nothing. Blaming it on being too overweight, she says she checked herself into a "fat farm" and used her obsession with the movie to try to lose the weight.

But her heart was heavy and tears poured out more often than not. Until one day, as she recounted in an interview with Larry King, she was finally able to *surrender*.

"I'm at this fat farm, praying and crying—saying to God, help me let this go. I wanted to be in this movie so much... I

thought I was going to be in the movie. There were all these signs that I was going to be in the movie... and as I'm on the track singing this song 'I surrender all, I surrender all—all to Thee my blessed Savior I surrender all.' A woman comes out to me and she says... 'There's a phone call for you.' And the phone call was Steven Spielberg saying, 'I want to see you in my office in California tomorrow.' That moment absolutely changed my life forever..."[3]

As I'm sure you know, Oprah got the part. Her career blossomed and ultimately burgeoned into the empire of influence it is now. But before any of that happened, a hurting, disappointed, weary young woman asked God to help her let her greatest desire—*go*. That's surrender. That's *how* you can surrender when you can't on your own.

She asked God to *help* her let it go.

Think about that—asking an all-powerful, all-knowing, all-able God to help you let go of your greatest desire is not a prayer I'm sure many of us pray, especially with regard to what we want most.

That's a bold prayer. That's a risky prayer. That's a do-whatever-it-takes prayer.

That's *surrender*.

Because anytime we pray in alignment with God's will, He promises to do it. So if giving up our deepest desire is what He wants, and we truly ask Him to help us do it, you bet He'll find a way. Now, I don't mean just

---

[3] https://www.youtube.com/watch?v=8EZZzhEOhig

mouthing the words so we can say we tried. I mean truly, truly asking Him to help us let go.

Whatever it takes, God, help me to surrender and let this go.

Is that a prayer you have prayed?

If you have, did you mean it?

That's a bold prayer. That's a risky prayer. That's a do-whatever-it-takes prayer.

Is that a prayer I prayed after my discussion with Dr. Bruce? Actually no, not right away. In fact, it would be seven long months from that late-night conversation before I would finally give up, get down on my knees and pray, "Whatever it takes, God. Help me let this go."

Whatever it takes? I heard a gentle whisper back.

"Yes, Lord, whatever it takes," I sighed, and I meant it.

Surrender Sets Free

Surrender is one of the major keys of answered prayer. This truth shows up all over the place. It's a phenomenon that couples who struggle to conceive will often do so only after they have surrendered to their inability and begin the process of adoption. Surrender opens more doors, and even wombs, than we can imagine. It is a powerful, life-changing, life-giving force.

Surrender allows us to dramatically reduce and even reverse the adverse physical, emotional and spiritual effects in our lives caused by anxiety, doubt, worry and fear. Surrender is necessary to give birth to faith in the areas of our greatest desires.

Yet it is also counter-intuitive to how we are challenged to live our lives. "Never give up, never surrender!" is the clarion call we hear on television, in films, sports and in history books. Refuse to surrender— our presidents, war heroes, activists and athletes urge us.

However, Christ modeled and spoke the opposite all the time praying, "Not my will, but Thy will be done." (Mark 14:36).

God challenges us to be "living sacrifices" (Romans 12:1), to "submit" ourselves to Him (James 4:7), and to consider ourselves with no more rights than a "slave" (Philippians 2:5-8). We are to "deny" ourselves—to the point of even taking up our own cross and following after Jesus (Luke 9:23-24) bearing His yoke in true surrender (Mathew 11:29). We are to develop and live out the mindset given in Galatians 2:20, "It is no longer I who live, but Christ who lives in me."

We are to surrender *all*.

Surrender is one of the major keys of answered prayer.

Especially those things we don't want to surrender *at all*.

And be aware; true surrender comes with pain, or it

isn't true surrender. That pain may be found only in the act of pronouncing our surrender—that initial process of relinquishing control in an area we desire greatly. Or it could come later through pain God uses to mold and shape us in order to bring about our answer. Or it could come in both. It also comes with fear, fear of losing what we really want God to provide.

Whatever the case, surrender requires a sacrifice that is real. Whether that sacrifice is in the mind, the will or the heart can differ depending on the situation. But sacrifice will be evident, and felt. If it's not then what you and I have done is more along the lines of agreeing, assenting or acquiescing. And that's very different from surrender.

Bear in mind, the sacrifice of surrender is also a different form of sacrifice than that which we often herald in our culture today. At times the sacrifices we applaud in ourselves and in others are not surrender at all. To give the lunch to the homeless person or the tithe when our bills are paid doesn't actually cost us much. To go the extra mile or be the devoted employee may be a sacrifice of sorts, but when we also look forward to the responses we believe it will bring or how it may make us feel, it's not surrender.

Surrender is necessary to give birth to faith in the areas of our greatest desires.

Only God Himself knows true surrender. Only He holds the scales and weighs them accurately. Scripture is replete with people who gave their lives in actions and activities of sacrifice that God did not count as worthy. We read about Pharisees who kept every law, those who crossed seas to make a convert, and even those who gave their bodies in sacrifice. Yet we also read it meant nothing in the kingdom economy because it was not coupled with humility, love or surrender.[4]

I imagine that when we get to heaven one day we will be surprised at how God measures true surrender. Those we held up as spiritual giants may not be seen as such up there. And then those we never even took a moment to notice may receive the greatest rewards.

True surrender is a pure abandonment of yourself at your core, for no other reason than to honor, obey and trust God. It is praying, and meaning, "Thy will be done." It is, as Dr. Bruce said so casually yet also so profoundly, being *okay* at the end of the day if only heaven is happy.

If only heaven is happy.

Oh friend, I wish you and I were sitting together right now. I wish we were sharing some time over a juice or a cup of coffee. Because I wish I could lean forward toward you at this moment, look you in the eyes, and ask you that question which so changed my life. Saying your name, I would then continue, "Are *you* okay with surrendering the thing you want most?"

It's an important question.

---

[4] Matthew 23:13, Matthew 23:15, 1 Corinthians 13:3

It's an essential question.

It's a question we all need to ask.

Are you *okay* if God never answers your prayer the way you truly want Him to?

It's a question we all need to ask.

That marriage you are praying for or that spouse who won't seem to connect, would you be *okay* if you were never emotionally restored, or worse yet he or she even left?

What about the health situation that continues to tap your energy, limit your abilities and bring you pain? Would you be *okay* if this is the best you ever feel again?

Or what about that job you desire or that one you want to leave? Would you be *okay* if you were never moved from where you work right now?

Or you never got promoted?

Or you always worked underneath that same, inattentive or overbearing boss?

Would you be *okay* living on the finances that are less than what you want?

Would you be *okay* never weighing less than what you weigh today?

Or never making the team?

Or getting that degree?

Or never catching the attention of the one who has caught yours?

Would you be *okay* if you never had a child?

Or a grandchild?

Or you never restored your relationship with your adult child, or parent or friend?

Would you be *okay* if you remained single for the rest of your life?

Are you *okay* if He never gives you, heals you, restores you or answers you in the way you most deeply want?

Be honest. It's just you and God.
Are you truly *okay* if only heaven is happy?
If you are not, then you may want to do what you probably don't want to do.
And that is ask God to help you surrender.
If you mean what you pray, you'll even give Him

permission to do whatever it takes to help you let go of what you are holding onto so dear. It's a scary prayer, I know. It's not a prayer we want to pray. But I promise you, if you cannot surrender—if I cannot surrender—the deepest desires we feel the most, our most precious *Isaacs*, then our prayers in those areas will always go unresolved.

If you are not, then you may want to do what you probably don't want to do. And that is ask God to help you surrender.

There is only one God in charge, and we are not Him. He gets to decide what is best for your life, and for mine. And we must trust, despite all we feel, think, and desire—that He ... knows ... best.

I understand if you are not ready to surrender right now. It took me seven searching months from the moment in the meeting room with Dr. Bruce to the moment on my knees in true surrender. It took mistakes. It took regrets. It took lessons learned.

It took actually hurting someone I cared deeply about who didn't deserve to be hurt through a wrong decision I made. It was a wrong decision driven solely by the distraction of my unresolved prayer. When I saw his pain I had caused, I knew I needed to come to grips with my own.

It is not always easy to realize how our internal

demons with whom we wrestle, our unmet desires and frustrated prayers, spill over to those around us in ways we never intended. Yet they do. They do through a shortness in our words, a lack of enthusiasm, a dryness in how we are relating, or even a judging tone. Our unresolved prayers impact our hearts, words and actions - negatively.

Other people deserve our entire involvement, presence, commitment, engagement, whatever it might be, whether friend, co-worker, or our family—in their lives. But it is other people who often get the short-end of what we have left over when our emotions and thoughts are tied up in our own desires, doubts and disappointments.

Surrender is a prayer with zero parameters and even less demands.

That's what happened with me. That's what finally woke me up. When I saw a poor choice I had made negatively impact someone who had done nothing to deserve my selfish decision, I knew I had to surrender. I realized I had to let this go.

Completely.

With no more strings attached to this prayer request.

Complete. Total. Surrender.

Surrender is a prayer with zero parameters and even less demands. It is a prayer from the authentic center of who you are. It doesn't have to be a long prayer. Truth needs no decor.

Peter's powerful, effective prayer as he sank beneath the literal waves of doubt was three words (Matthew 14:30). God knows what you mean the moment your knees hit the floor, and honestly—He knows even before.

A prayer of surrender is a prayer of alignment.

As importantly, it is also a prayer of release. Surrender is a gentle shift in your way of *being*, allowing you to let go of anxious attachments and clingy expectations. It removes attempts to make something happen regarding your desired outcome. It stops you from resorting to what I call, "pulling a Hagar"—trying to *make* things happen outside of God's plan, all the while winding up with a whole lot of mess instead.[5]

Surrender is a prayer that enables you and I to be free to be all God wants us to be—a soul used by Him at the maximum level to receive His love and to love others.

Maybe you are ready to surrender. Or maybe you are just ready to ask God to help you in that direction.

If you are, you can pray a simple prayer like this,

"Lord, You are in charge. I give You permission— no, I give You an invitation—to do whatever it takes to shift my spirit into alignment with Yours. Even if

---

[5] See the story in Genesis 16 when Abraham and Sarah believed God's promise for a son but saw no movement toward that promise. Trying to force their desire into creation, Sarah offered her husband to connect with Hagar so that her handmaid could bear them a son. This led to centuries of conflict between two people groups, even to this day.

that means pain. Even if that means causing me to release a desire I can't imagine living without. Even if that means loss. Even if that means anything at all that I don't even know to fear ahead of time.

Do it because it's more important to me that my heart beats in cadence with Your own. When it does, I will love you more boldly, love others more purely (Matthew 22:37-40) and receive the resolutions to my prayers – whether yes, no or wait. Limbo will no longer be my normal. So Lord, please help me to let this specific desire go (*yes, name it*), trusting You for what is best. Even if it's a no."

That, my friend, is a bold prayer.
That is a warrior's prayer.
That is a victor's prayer.
And yes, I know, that is a frightening prayer.
Yet no one ever conquered fear with courage. Courage only masks it. Fear is conquered through faith alone. Faith that as you, and I, wade into the depths of this unknown spirit called surrender, God *will* meet us, keep us, provide for us and make us truly *okay* in those moments, minutes – even months or more - when only heaven is happy.

Will you surrender all?

CHAPTER 5: A CUP OR A SMILE

Surrender is the key to accepting answered prayer. But how can you tell if you have truly surrendered? One way is to let your actions and thoughts inform you.

Do you keep journaling about the same thing?

Do you keep going back to God in prayer for the same thing?

Do you have a nagging feeling inside of you about the same thing?

Do your comments spill over into your relationships, words and actions coming out as complaints, frustration or emptiness due to this same thing?

Do you keep living your life in "wait" mode, as if your current situation is not enough for you to be perfectly at peace, present and content?

God gave me a visual illustration of what authentic surrender looks like a while back. It helped me to recognize the difference between cognitive surrender and surrender from my soul. Two ladies had approached me at church prior to the service. They introduced themselves as part of the prayer ministry and then asked if I had a prayer request. Of course I did, I thought. The reason I thought that was because at this time in my life, this "thing," this prayer request, was constantly on my mind. So I told them what it was and asked if they could pray that God would give me a sign as to His answer.

Surrender is the key to accepting answered prayer.

The ladies prayed, and one in particular asked God to give me the sign right there that morning. Not two minutes later, Priscilla, the actress from the movie I mentioned earlier, walked by. She placed her hand on my shoulder as she passed my pew and said hello. We exchanged a few words, after which I asked, "Are you excited about August?" August was when the movie she starred in was going to be released.

A look of pure unknowing covered her face as she responded, "What's happening in August?"

I smiled, knowing that was my sign for which the ladies had prayed. After all, it's not every day that someone gets to star in their very first movie. Seeing yourself on the big screen and knowing you are impacting so many people in such an enormous way would be a pretty important thing to most of us. And yet, here was Priscilla—so content and caught up in her everyday life and in being at church that something most of us would consider to be enormous had slipped her mind.

"*War Room?*" I replied, "It comes out in August."

Priscilla smiled, then answered, "Oh yes, I'm excited—I had just forgotten, that's all."

What a reminder to me, and to all of us, of the value of "forgetting." Priscilla didn't have to *will* the movie to come out in August. She didn't have to *force* it. She didn't have to *worry* it into existence, or even bemoan its lack of existence while she waited. If it wasn't even on her mind when asked about it, I can bet it wasn't the first thing she offered as a prayer request either—that it would, indeed, be released in August. The movie was going to come out because the movie was going to come out. The people who had created it had made a plan. It would release in August. Priscilla's awareness of that truth is a picture of what surrender really looks like.

Far too often, we worry, fret, think about and pray over that which we are *not* confident will come about. And yet the secret to living a life of surrender actually comes in the forgetting—in the letting go—being confident that the One who created us has made a plan. And that it's a good plan, with a future filled with hope.

In that confidence, we are to ask our requests.

Then forget. And let go.

Let me illustrate it another way. Around that same time, my daughter was about to get married. As the wedding planner for her big day, I had become intimately acquainted with the postal office workers, the FedEx delivery drivers and the UPS drivers as well. They had delivered boxes upon boxes upon boxes to my home containing everything from candles and chair sashes to lightsaber centerpieces (it was a Star Wars and movie themed wedding). You would think Willie Wonka was throwing the reception by the amount of candies, lollipops and licorice I had as well. Thank God for Etsy and the Internet!

Yet as these brown paper packages all tied up with strings kept coming to my home, I will admit that I never once spent any of my time wondering if they would arrive. Once I ordered whatever it was online, I let it go.

I didn't fret. I didn't check UPS tracking. I didn't even wonder what day each item would come. It's not because I didn't care. I really did care, deeply. Each item had been hand-picked with love and ordered from trusted websites whose reviews I had read before placing my order. I didn't request anything from anyone with bad reviews. Why would I?

In that confidence, we are to ask our requests. Then forget. And let go.

But the same faith I put in my vendors for my daughter's wedding ought to be the same faith I put in God with regard to needs I have that only He can meet. After all, He's got impeccable reviews, too. Prayers done

His way, according to His prescribed approach, always get replies. If a prayer gets no reply, it's not because He has fallen short, but rather it is because we have asked awry.

Surrender means trusting that what I need is what I'll get—that what is promised will be delivered, and, simply, that God knows what is best. If my request is wrong, God will say, "No." If my timing is wrong, God will say, "Slow." Surrender involves a willingness to accept both.

Surrender Isn't Simple

I'll admit it, though, surrender isn't simple. Sometimes we can choose to surrender without it actually resonating as truth in our hearts. I've done that. Maybe you have too. The evening after I had met with Dr. Bruce, our church was having another service. That night's message involved each of us in the congregation going forward to place an offering in the baskets on the altar. The offering was supposed to come from a true heart of sacrifice. Bruce had been encouraging us all week long to give our time, talents and treasures to the Lord, over and above what we felt comfortable doing.

God already had my time, I mused. I was single; He had all my time. So I didn't really feel the need to commit any more to Him in that area. But the one thing God did not have entirely, I knew, was a heart of surrender in this prayer request in my life: of letting go of what I thought I wanted most—a healthy marriage relationship.

So when it came time to put our offerings in the baskets, I went forward with everyone else. But instead of money, I put in a ring. It was a ring I had purchased a few years earlier as a symbol to pray for and hope for a loving marriage someday. Thus, in the basket went my ring; back to the pew went me.

There, I did it God. I surrendered. Or so I thought. Not long after my beautiful ring got placed in the basket, God ushered a very plainly dressed older woman, who was not wearing a wedding ring either, to sit down right next to me. If anyone looked like the lonely, single, nun-like stereotypical maid, it would have been her.

I shuddered.

Yes, shuddered.

Why, God?

Why, after I surrendered my hope for a mate to You, did You usher this poor, lonely woman to sit next to me. Couldn't You have brought me a prince instead? After all, I surrendered!

God whispered in reply, *You may have put the ring in the basket, my dear—but you have not surrendered.*

"How do You know I have not surrendered, God?" I asked, now very frustrated with the whole experience. I debated whether there was a way to retrieve my ring from the basket if things were going to continue down this line.

I know you have not surrendered, Heather, because of how you responded to the lady next to you. I saw your response. You did, too. You refuse to end up like her. And that is not surrender.

He was right.

He always is.

I hadn't surrendered this prayer to Him.

Surrender means trusting that what I need is what I'll get—that what is promised will be delivered, and, simply, that God knows what is best.

Even though I had given God what I thought was my surrender—it really wasn't surrender at all. It was more of a ploy to let Him think I had surrendered in hopes that maybe He would then—finally—answer my prayer the way I wanted Him to.

Ever tried something similar? We all do. These are actions of surrender and words of surrender—trying to convince others and God, and even ourselves, that we have truly surrendered.

But God isn't tricked by our actions or our words. He knows our hearts—even more than we do. And sometimes He has to reveal that truth to us so we won't live under a false reality that we are someone we are not. Because if we live in this false reality, we will never get around to what we must do—surrender.

And without surrender, we will never get around to answered prayer in the areas we want the most.

Why? Because "without faith it is impossible to please God." (Hebrews 11:6) Faith says, "I trust You. I put all my eggs in Your basket. I put my ring in your basket. I surrender my desires beneath Your will. I trust that whatever I give up, go without, sacrifice or lack—because of my trust in You, Lord—You will either give it back, You will release me from the desire for it, or You will give me something more."

Getting It Back

I once had a red suit coat hanging in my closet.

It was a size too big, but I wore it for years. Mostly as a reminder. A memory. A testimony of greater things.

I had gotten my jacket from a used clothing store on the campus of the seminary I attended at the time. I suppose I shouldn't really call it a store since the clothes there were free. They had been donated to the seminary for the use of the students and their families. Probably rounded up by those who had once attended there themselves and who knew the impossibility of working, schooling and providing for a family all at one time. So they thought they might help out by at least donating their clothes.

I had gone one day to pick out a few things for a new job. I was about to start as a teacher in a local Christian high school. I had wanted some suit coats to go with my skirts, but I had only found this one. I liked it, though, even if, as I said, it was a size too large.

But God isn't tricked by our actions or our words. He knows our hearts.

Now, for this next part of the story, it might be good for you to keep in mind that the seminary used to be one of the grandest in the land. It was built in the most beautiful of locations in the heart of Dallas. But that was a few years ago. Okay, really that was a few decades ago.

And cities change over time. So at the time of this particular occurrence, it was located in what most would consider the slums. It was a dangerous area where theft was commonplace. The seminary faculty told all of the incoming students not to hand out money to any beggars, to lock your car at all times, and not to walk alone off the premises of the campus.

Yes, I had been warned.

But then I saw her.

She stood next to a shopping cart that had definitely seen brighter days. It leaned, as if somehow given to a limp on its right, front side. The frail, weather-beaten woman standing next to it didn't look much better herself. Lines carved themselves into what once was soft, smooth and hopeful skin, etching reminders of pain, loss and neglect.

Her shopping cart sunk under the weight of what must have been her entire collection of belongings. They were bundled in plastic bags, stacked one on top of each other. A hand-made sign hung from the front of her rusty cart. It had been written with a marker on a piece of cardboard.

It read, "Crosses For Money"

My eyes shifted to the crosses dangling from her cart. Apparently, she had made them out of yarn and plastic. Where had she sat when she had made them, I wondered? In a shelter? On the street? On a bench?

I didn't know.

When she was younger, had she hoped someday that she would grow up and make crosses out of yarn? Is that what her heart had dreamed of? I didn't think so.

I imagined she must have been a lot like me and dreamed of dancing or being a ballerina or an ice skater or a singer or a lawyer or a broadcaster —anything we girls are so naturally drawn to—that gives life and beauty back into this world.

But somehow, somewhere along the lines now creasing her brow, life had taught her that she couldn't do it. That she wouldn't make it. That she couldn't finish school. Or get the guy. Or make the grades. Or keep the job. Or stop the drinking. Or ease the pain.

Or cover the shame.

Or be beautiful once again.

Somewhere along the lines carved deeply in her soul, lies had replaced truth. And, what's worse, she had believed them.

The woman didn't say anything to me when I looked directly at her. She couldn't. My window was up. My door was locked. I had been told that that's how it should be in this part of town.

But there she stood with a shopping basket decked out in hand-made crosses woven with yarn and a weathered cardboard sign.

For some reason, the stop light in front of me remained red for a suspicious length of time. Red like the suit coat I had just picked up – for free, the one a size too large. The thought of giving this woman money came to me, but it was quickly chased by the next one: What money, Heather? I never had any cash on hand. We were living on a thousand dollars a month ourselves, with a family of five. I no longer even carried a billfold or purse because there really wasn't any point. Money? Right.

But on this day God had planned ahead. On this day, I opened the ash tray just in case, in order to see if there was any change to give and there it was—a crisp five-dollar bill. Guilt struck me at first when I felt myself processing the thought that, *Wow, five dollars is an awful lot of money to give away*. I wished it had only been one or two dollars.

I can't give away five dollars, I thought. *That's too much.*

But it was all I had.

So I quickly grabbed the five-dollar bill, unlocked my door, dashed out, and handed it to the woman with the shopping cart covered with crosses made of yarn. She still didn't say a word. Her smile formed—the kind of smile where the lips move but the heart stays still and the eyes look as lost as ever. I couldn't look at her anymore.

So I chose the purple one.

Then I hopped back in my car, mumbling a thank you and glad it was done.

An hour passed and I was back home. I was happy that I had given the woman my money but I was also wondering where I would get the money for what we needed that week too. Five dollars was a lot of money to us at that time. Attempting to lift my spirits, I went into my room and tried on my "new" used clothes. I put on my oversized red jacket and looked in the mirror.

It was big, yet it would do well. I was grateful.

But then I put both of my hands into the pockets, because that way you couldn't really tell that the sleeves went down past my wrists—and I thought, *Well, I could just walk around like this when I wear it.*

Yet when I stuck my hands in the pockets, I felt something. It felt like paper. Maybe an old receipt from the previous owner, I didn't know. I decided to find out so I pulled it out. And there it was—a five-dollar bill. It wasn't a twenty. It wasn't even a one.

It was exactly what I had just given to the woman with the purple cross. Some busy soul must have forgotten about this five-dollar bill when she had donated the red jacket to the seminary.

But God hadn't.

He hadn't forgotten.

He knew all along.

And He knew just how much I would need it.

Not for milk. Nor for diapers.

He knew I needed it for my soul.

I needed it as a reminder that God is never late nor ever lacking when we abide by His will. God promises:

Delight yourself in the Lord;
And He will give you the desires of your heart.
Commit your way to the Lord,
Trust also in Him and He will do it.
Psalm 37:4, 5

But what if there hadn't been a five-dollar bill in my red coat pocket? Would God still be good?

Yes, He would.

Because sometimes God gives us exactly what we

think we need. But other times, He doesn't. And if we'll only learn to look for Him in the midst of the "no" or of the "wait," He can, in those times, actually give us more. What do I mean?

Getting More

We discover this truth in another story about another beggar who sat nearby a seminary of sorts during his day. This man didn't have a shopping cart with crosses hung from it, but he was just as hungry, just as weary and just as empty as the woman I had met.

What's worse is that this man was also handicapped, surrounded by the spiritual success stories of his day. The place he had chosen to beg was a place for the beautiful. In fact, it was a gate called Beautiful, crafted from ornate stone and elegantly designed. This gate opened to a world of the elite, pampered and well-to-do. Daily, they would pass through this gate on their way to pay homage to the One who had made them that way. Worry lines and furrowed brows had been washed away in private baths, oil treatments, facials and massages. A fragrant aroma of costly perfumes wafted in the air, only to collide with the beggar's own stench having not bathed in what had obviously been far too long.

But there he sat each day at this gate—a gate called Beautiful. He was a man who had never known what beautiful truly was. In his hand he held his cup. And in his cup rested a few coins—coins that the beautiful people had dropped in earlier that day. It wasn't enough for dinner quite yet.

So he sat, among the stares. He had long gotten used to the stares. He had long gotten used to the others who didn't stare but rather treated him as if he didn't even exist. People's reactions made no difference to him anymore. What mattered was if he would eat. That's all that mattered. That was his deepest need.

That was his prayer.

That was the thing he would have written about had he the paper to journal.

That was the thing he kept going back to God to ask.

That was the nagging feeling inside him day in and day out, gnawing at his gut – literally.

That was the subject of all his conversations, complaints and frustrations.

That was what held him in a continual state of want.

That was the thing that made peace and contentment elusive goals at best.

This man needed to eat like he needed to breathe. And yet, he had no way to meet his need on his own. He had no way to answer his prayer on his own. He had no job, no income—he had no hope.

So when two men came up to him later in the day and told him to look at them but then went on to say that they had no money to give, I imagine his heart must have sunk. Why would two perfectly healthy and well-clothed men ask a beggar to look at them? Why would they tell him that they didn't have the one thing that he needed the most? Wasn't that more cruel than just walking by? Wouldn't that be more like taunting?

But one of these men kept on talking.

"I do not possess silver and gold," he said, "but what I do have I give to you: In the name of Jesus Christ the Nazarene—walk!" (Acts 3:3-10).

What?

Walk.

The man's aching muscles must have felt a shimmer of courage at the thought. But how could he walk if he couldn't even stand? That's when one of the men reached out and offered him his hand. And then the crippled man did a very, very brave thing. He set down his cup and grabbed ahold of the hand. After he did, his legs and feet were immediately strengthened.

How do I know? Because not only did this lame man start to walk, but he also danced!

You might be wondering what a crippled beggar has to do with us and our wish lists and unresolved prayers. A lot, actually. In fact—everything. Because even though we may feel we know what we really need, God knows best.

He sees you and me sitting there empty, spent, tired and worn out. He knows our pain. He knows our hunger. He knows that thought that dominates all others. He knows we hurt as we watch people walk by living the life we desire. He sees us scrolling through social media page after social media page, envying the so-called perfect lives others got but we somehow missed out on.

He sees your heart - you who have no child as you watch other parents post pictures of theirs.

He sees your soul single woman as you go through yet another Valentine's Day or weekend alone.

He hears your heaving sigh from your frail body as you wonder how healthy people can take their health for granted.

He feels your emptiness married husband or wife, drowning in a sea of disappointment envying other couples nearby.

He knows that it is not only the woman with the shopping basket, the greyed hair and the worn face sitting along the gate to the seminary called Beautiful.

He knows that it is not only the lame man with the rough face and the mismatched clothes sitting on the ground at the gate called Beautiful.

He knows that you and I are sitting there too, with hearts as empty as a beggar's cup and carts burdened under the weight of lost desires.

Our legs may be fine, but our hopes are hurt. Our bank accounts may be full, but our dreams are empty. Our faces are worn with a painted on smile. We beg for anything that might make the pain of this unresolved prayer … simply …. go … away.

He knows that you and I are sitting there too, with hearts as empty as a beggar's cup.

Oh, yes, we live in a modern world, so our begging takes on modern forms, but we still do it. Many of us still do it. We beg at the mall with "retail therapy." We beg with books, movies or television shows that input something into our senses that we feel is missing in our lives. We beg with diet pills, wrinkle creams, too much exercise or careers for the sole purpose of finding a distraction to numb our ache. We beg with purses in every color, shoes in every style, sporting teams with names of players we wear on our own backs. We beg with too much coffee. Too much cake. Too much wine. Porn. Gossip. Sex. We beg in so many ways.

Anything to fill up our little cup of needs not met.

Yes, we *even* pray.

But all the while, God stands before us asking us to put our eyes on Him. To look toward Him. He stares down at us—no—He crouches. Can you see Him crouching now? I do. He's kneeling, and gazing right into your eyes. Into my eyes. He's there, and He's saying,

"My dear sweet love, I'm not going to give you what you think you need right now—because, honestly, you need a whole lot more. If I gave you what you were asking for, you'd be back here begging again tomorrow. It can't fill you. It won't satisfy you. You need to first learn how to stand on your own. Just you, and Me. Right now. Right here. In this dirty, pit of a place that is actually (if you will but open your eyes) – actually Beautiful.

Take My hand, my dear one. You need to first discover that you are strong enough – good enough – whole enough, without anything else.

Without anyone else, but Me.

My delightful one, *YOU* must know how to dance alone before you can ever keep step with another. You must learn that *YOU* are beautiful before you'll ever receive the love of another. *You* are able. *You* are well. *You* are forgiven. *You* are accepted. *You* are safe. *You* are significant. *You* are whole. Because I am all of this, and more. And you are with Me.

After speaking such truths to your soul, God's hand then reaches out to lift you, and me, from our dust. From our pit. From our beggar's position of need. But He won't force us. He won't make us set down our cup. That's up to you. That's up to me.

But one thing I do know is, we can't have both. We can't keep the cup in our hand while holding onto His. We must choose.

If we choose the cup because we trust the coins since that's all we've ever known, He will let us keep it. But it's all we'll ever know. And each day will simply mirror the one before—an empty cup waiting to be filled back up again.

But if we set our cup down and grab His hand, we won't need to look to others for coins anymore. Remember what the crippled man did when he stood? I'll tell you what he didn't do - he didn't start looking for coins.

No, he danced.

He had better things to do than to wait for others to meet his needs. He had the strength now to meet his own. And if that truth – that possibility doesn't make you dance, I don't know what will.

To see God provide for and satisfy our souls, our needs, our wants and desires in ways we couldn't have anticipated is the greatest gift of all. To see Him teach us about who we really are and what we really need matters more and lasts longer than any answered prayer.

Dancing doesn't mean you no longer want the answer that you prayed for before. Learning to dance means you no longer *need* it.

There's a big difference in that.

Through surrender, God opens our eyes to the sufficiency of our lives in Him. It is in that space that we can clarify our desires because when we are needy, clingy or desperate for an answer – the root behind what we want is often clouded by emotion, and our desire may not even be entirely true.

Let me explain through personal vulnerability. Since the time of my "surrender" of this prayer request, I was given the mental and emotional space to discover some of the reasons this particular prayer wasn't answered way-back-when with what's-his-name for me. Reasons that had previously been hidden under the weight of my perceived need and strong emotions of not wanting to be alone another day longer. I couldn't see them or recognize them before.

For example, in two decades of an "intense" marriage relationship that fostered my "dependence", I had forgotten how innately "independent" I truly am. I had unlearned that trait. But in all honesty, I actually enjoy my freedom, flexibility and even my own space. In these years I've spent alone – traveling all over the world alone many times, I've been reminded that as a child I regularly sought out independence and time to myself – something that can be hard to come by in a marriage relationship.

On a lighter note, but no less important, I also discovered that I truly enjoy not having to share a closet, bathroom, schedule or even having to run my choices for dinner, vacations, spending, movies – whatever - through someone else's grid.

I came to realize that there was a lot about being single that I really did enjoy. I didn't realize it before because I was so consumed with getting that "prayer request" answered for what I thought I needed. But God knew I needed to learn to be whole on my own – completely complete as a single – or I would wind up in an unhealthy, dependency-based relationship rather than a purely mutual, healthy marriage.

Make sense? You might be able to apply the principle of what I learned to a situation you are facing, even if the details aren't identical. Because while this isn't a book on dating, let me explain that once I surrendered and was able to gain the emotional space necessary for true clarity about my authentic wants and desires, I discovered that while my emotions may have wanted my prayer answered all those years, my subconscious beliefs and desires really did not. My subconscious beliefs and desires were for a mutually-healthy independent, yet inter-locking, relationship. And until I was able to get to that place myself in my own healing and maturity, the types of men I would be attracted to would fall in the other category – not the category I wanted and needed most.

Not until I could reach a space of clarity and wholeness first would I then look for a partner who embodied wholeness as well.

Thus, I wasn't in alignment with what I really wanted internally when I prayer all those years because what I needed (my subconscious spirit knew) wasn't what my emotions felt I needed (to close the gap immediately on being alone). And until the body, mind and spirit agree (remember that passage about praying in spirit and truth?) getting an answered prayer could wind up being a very wrong answer.

Unanswered prayer gives us time. Time to understand what we really want. Or, what we really need. And what areas in our own life we may need to work on in order to be strong enough and ready to handle rightly our answered prayer.

For me, this time alone where God had seemingly not "answered my prayer for a mate" helped me to realize that there were valid (and invalid) reasons I didn't date quickly, or much at all. Some of those reasons were healthy and some required healing, sure, but the root was real. To ignore that root would mean "settling" just to get my prayer answered.

But that's what we do, isn't it? When we obsess about our prayer requests rather than trust that God knows best we will seek (like Abraham with Hagar) to **settle** for a solution rather than seek God's provision.

After which, we regret it for years, even decades. Only surrender frees us from the risk of *settling*.

Have you ever heard the phrase, "Thank God for unanswered prayer"? It's truth because our emotions will often lead us to pray for things we don't really even want (or may not be ready yet to receive in our own development). Which if we get it, can turn into a disaster.

God knows us better than we know ourselves and sometimes our emotions are so strong, our triggers so tender and our felt needs so deep we forget who we truly are and what we *truly* need. All the while God is saying,

> "Trust me, I know what is best for you. I know what you really want. And it's not the coins in the cup. My child, you need more than the coins in that cup. You need to be whole first."

Whatever your prayer is—whether it revolves around a job, your health, a family member, an addictive behavior, your finances, your past—your present. Whatever it is you think you may need, remember that God might have something greater in His hand for you. But He needs you whole first.

If He is not giving you the answer you seek right now, He might be trying to lift your sight from your empty cup up to Him. He may be holding out His hand to lift you in a way that will develop you to have the strength, dignity and confidence in yourself you need and identity in Him.

Unanswered prayer is a teacher, teaching us one thing, if we will but listen: Endurance. And endurance produces strength of character, and strength of character produces hope (Romans 5:4). God is after your personal growth and refinement as your loving Father.

What does it mean when prayer gets no reply?

What I learned in those years of reflection is that my first prayer-marathon worked in that long-ago dating scenario but not my second because I viewed the first dissolving of the relationship to a one-time thing – a mistake, misunderstanding, etc. My mind was still invested and able to trust, entirely. I gave the benefit of the doubt.

But when the second situation happened that raised the repeated red flag, even I couldn't deceive myself any longer. Just like our adrenaline kicks in during "fight or flight," designed to protect us with extra strength – our sub-conscious blocks our belief when we recognize what we thought we wanted isn't exactly what we thought it was after all. Yes – my emotions wanted the "us" back. My heart wanted the relationship to work but my mind knew better. Sometimes your heart has to accept what your mind already knows. But that can take time. On the second situation, my spirit and my mind decided it was best to protect myself by no longer believing the relationship was solvent and healthy. It heeded the red flags everyone else had tried to show me.

Even though I prayed with fervency and desired it greatly, my mind and my spirit knew it was better to protect me by no longer signing off on the relationship.

Thus, I no longer believed it was something I *should* want. At least not internally.

When this happens, it's always best not to follow your heart but rather – to listen to your mind and your spirit. Yes, you may still feel the feelings but you have to choose to let go. The feelings will follow.

See, our minds have been wired to protect us. Our subconscious has been wired that way as well. Did you know that when you are sleeping – soundly sleeping – your subconscious can still hear dangerous threats that may be taking place and wake you up? Our subconscious beliefs actually determine a lot of what we accomplish in life. Getting them in alignment with the beliefs you are aware of is essential to answered prayer.

What does that mean when we pray only with our emotions and heart, but not our mind/will? It means we don't really want the answer to our prayer after all. We are no longer praying in "spirit and truth." Because the truth in my spirit knew by then that I did not want to be in a relationship that showed no real evidence of spiritual alignment. Even though "I" wanted to no longer be single desperately.

Thus, my prayers conflicted internally.

Friend, I don't think we pay enough attention to our internal beliefs, thoughts and even our subconscious truth. But we should. It's our body's way of guiding us when our emotions are too strong and too volatile to guide us wisely (which emotions are rarely what guides us wisely anyhow.)

If your prayer is not getting answered in the way you want, take some time to focus inward. Meditate on what matters most. Get honest with yourself. After all, you may be wiser than you think. And your subconscious spirit-based beliefs may be protecting you from getting something you don't really want, or shouldn't have.

It also may mean that your "fight or flight" mechanism has been activated internally. When that's the case, you will need to spend time meditating and focusing on truth in order to re-align your subconscious beliefs with what your awareness believes. You will need to pray and ask God for wisdom on how to heal and grow spiritually so that your emotions/mind align with your spirit. Part of the process to unlocking the key to getting the answers to your prayers you want the most is aligning your internal beliefs with your external ones. Do that and you have your answer.

But what else does it really mean when prayer gets no reply? It also means it simply didn't get the reply you, or I, had originally wanted OR emotionally thought we wanted. Because prayer *always* gets a reply. God promises to never leave us nor forsake us. He promises to meet all of our needs according to His riches in glory. He promises that no good thing will be withheld from you, or me, when we love Him.

God promises to reply:

> *Call to Me and I **will** answer you.*
> *Jeremiah 33:3*

He may not answer with a coin in your cup, or a five-dollar bill in your pocket. Or even a mate and a marriage. Or a child. A job. Finances. Restored health. But He will answer with what you, and I, need most at this particular time. Sometimes simply learning that we can stand on our own—without the exact thing we have been praying for, hungry for, or even desperate for—*is the best answer of all.*

In learning this, we find out how to fill our own cups first. Because going through life as a beggar isn't really that beautiful at all. No matter how many coins in your cup you wind up with. At the end of the day, you still have to beg again tomorrow.

Yet when we experience the clarity that true awareness through surrender provides, we will no longer settle for just any random coin. Or just any random passerby. Or just any answered prayer.

We will no longer try to force our own answers either, ignoring limiting beliefs and internal hesitations. Rather, we will be too busy dancing in the Beauty of our own strength to do any of that because being made whole—being made strong—is pretty great all on its own.

And while we dance, we may just forget about that unanswered prayer. Or we may not. It could be a timing thing as we grow and as our soul shifts through personal strength into the best possible position for answered prayer—a position of ongoing hope rooted in trust. After all, hope is a great place from which to pray, " … and hope does not disappoint …." (Romans 5:5)

Remember my unicorn at the start of this book? Remember how I used it as a reminder to me of what kind of mindset in which to pray? And how it worked?

Friend, when you discover the Beauty of personal wholeness through the power of pure surrender, you will naturally pray with a unicorn frame-of-mind, even for those things you desire most.

You will pray from a position of strength.

It all started with a unicorn and a rainbow.

A simple idea. I had learned over time that when we pray, we should be mindful of the attitude and spirit in which we pray. Always pray from a position of gratitude and joy rather than desperation and lack. Gratitude and joy demonstrate faith. And God adores faith. Faith is God's love language.

The idea in prayer is to get creative—have fun with it. Prayer doesn't have to be ritualistic, boring or even all that religious.

God is real. Talk to Him like He is real.

*Talk to Him like you know Him, and you'll be surprised how much He makes Himself known. Do whatever you need to do to give yourself a mindset of happiness and **hope** when you pray. Then sit back and watch Him move mountains on your behalf.*

Even if that mountain just happens to be - *You*.
It is then you will experience the unveiling, stripping

and aligning power of surrender. It is then you will discover the cadence of a brand new dance.

And, frankly, it is often then – at the point of surrender – when you no longer feel like you need, need, need, need the object of your prayer's desire – that God gives you what you wanted all along.

It's after letting go that He lets us have it.

Nearly two years passed since I had surrendered – I had spent those years seeking to heal past wounds stretching decades deep and mature spiritually. Essentially, I invested heavily in my own personal growth. By doing so, I reached a place of pure contentment. I enjoyed my life, I was no longer "bored," I spent more time with my kids, reading, focusing on work – traveling – you name it. I laughed a lot. Sure, the thought of this ongoing lack of a marriage and mate crept up every once in a while, but I honestly thought God had asked me to give that up – to surrender. So I would simply recognize the thought, let it go and move on.

Even though I was disappointed to still be single, I was content. It's a unique space to be in where your desire wasn't met but you really are "okay" with it.

Then one day a friend shared with me how she had made a list after a decade of singlehood of everything she had wanted in a mate. And she told me how she had dug a hole and stuck the list in the ground and planted a tree in that spot. And lo and behold, God had literally brought her the man to whom she was now married just a few months later. It was a whirlwind romance and they both serve in full-time ministry now.

I thought ... "A list?" I had never made a list.
Seemed silly. A **wish list**, I guess. But okay, why not. So I
grabbed my journal and first prayed something of the
sort:

"Dear God, I know I have surrendered so if You
don't want to give me a husband – I'm perfectly okay
with that – and You know that. But if You do – I
want to make sure the husband You give me won't
take away from any of the work I do for you – but
will actually help me serve You more, as I will help
him too. That's my main condition. And these are
the things I hope for in him as a person."

I then turned to my journal and wrote 20 very
specific things. Why not? God is a big God after all. I
reflected on how He had brought in nearly to the dollar
amount what I had put on my unicorn posters each year
for work. Why not get just as specific about what I
wanted in a husband as I had done then? This, after all,
was far more important to me. So I did. I wrote an entire
page. I then put my "wish list" away and honestly forgot
about my list (and my prayer) because I had truly
surrendered after all.

Not six weeks later, a dear friend from high school –
whom I had worked with when we were teens 30 years
earlier– reached out. We hadn't seen each other since
high school. He had been shy back then and even though
he had a crush on me (which was adorably obvious back
then), he had never acted on it. Well, he wasn't shy

anymore.

His son had graduated as Valedictorian from high school – it was his second son to be given the honor – so I commented on his Facebook post "Congrats." I know – eloquent. He then messaged me to ask if he could call. I said, "Sure – you've got ten minutes as I run to the store." Goodness, okay – so flirting isn't my strength.

He later told me that when I said he had ten minutes, he thought, "I better make this good."

He did just that because ten minutes turned into three hours. Sounds trite, but I can honestly say we fell in love that first week. Less than a year later, we were married. Just ten months after making my detailed "wish list" – we stood at the altar in front of family and friends and truly had the fairy tale ceremony.

When it came time for us to pack up and move to a new house, I ran across that "wish list." I had totally forgotten about it. I thought – wow, let's see how close he actually is to what I was thinking. I knew I couldn't be more happy than I was with him but I wondered how many things on the list actually came about.

I was alarmed!

After all, it had been a fun little project so I had been very specific. And, yes, he had nailed 19 of the 20 things on the list. No joke. I quickly showed it to him. And the one thing he didn't nail, he probably will in the near future – that one actually takes time to cross off.

But what's more – by the time I had written that list, I had written as a ghostwriter probably close to a thousand guided prayers in multiple guided prayer books.

So one of the specific things on my list I had put was that I wanted a man who would initiate prayer and pray with, for and over me and us daily. I didn't want to carry that spiritual burden in addition to all I had already invested emotionally and spiritually into penning so many prayers for others. I wanted a man who would carry that for us, lead me in prayer, guide me and own that for us as a couple.

Yet without ever mentioning it to him, and even forgetting it was even on my list, he had initiated our daily prayers only a few weeks into our dating relationship. He started by writing them out. He would spend over an hour at times typing them on his computer and then send them to me. We would also pray them together over the phone. They were/are beautiful. Heartfelt. I've saved every one.

Yes, Jack had me at "Dear Lord God ...."

What's more, after we married, those lengthy, beautiful regular prayers have only continued and increased. There it was – my desire for a husband who would lead us in regular prayers - right on my wish list. Item after item after item. He was all of that, and even so much more than I could have or ever did hope for.

In showing me my "Wish List" God made it clear:

Heather, when you surrender to Me and are in alignment under Me and stop your complaining, obsessing, yearning and wishing – rather, simply give your wish list to Me and forget about it – so you can focus on what I want you to do and who I want you to be to advance my glory on earth and grow spiritually – when you do that, I got you covered. I'll take care of that Wish List – plus more.

And He did just that. My heart is fuller than I've ever known. Yet before it could reach this place, my heart had to be emptied first – emptied of the entitlement, doubt and contradictions. Those things which block our prayers and keep us from alignment in body, mind and spirit with God's truth. My heart had to surrender and let go of what I thought I needed most so that I could be truly "okay" when only heaven was happy.

That's surrender.

That's the secret to answered prayer.

Will you choose to surrender? Will you think about that one thing – or several – that you are truly seeking resolution in your life about, and lay it before the Lord in surrender? Then, after you do, write out your own version of a "wish list" whether it be for your health, work, family, fun, calling, marriage or more. Get specific. He is a detailed kind-of God. Then, let it go. Move on. Enjoy each day in His presence and purpose, trusting Him with the desires of your heart through true surrender.

10109680R00073

Made in the USA
Middletown, DE
11 November 2018